Der Turner Soldat;

A Turner Soldier in the Civil War;

Germany to A

A Biographical Narrative of a German Immigrant who served as a Private in the 20th Regiment, New York Volunteers, The United Turner Rifles.

A Commemorative Work for the
125th Anniversary of the American Civil War

by

C. Eugene Miller Ph.D.
Professor of Engineering Mechanics
University of Louisville
Louisville, Kentucky

and

Forrest F. Steinlage L.S.
National Historian
The American Turners
Louisville, Kentucky

Calmar Publications

Louisville, Kentucky

Erhard Futterer (der Turner Soldat). He was born August 30, 1831 at Forchheim, Baden, emigrated to America in 1855, and served as a private in Company B, 20th New York Regiment, the United Turner Rifles during the Civil War. After the war, he settled in Buffalo, New York, and died there on March 6, 1889. Photograph taken by Merz and Ulrich, 185 Essex Street, New York City, 1864.

DEDICATION

To you, the descendants of the 19th century Turners and Acht-und-vierziger, we dedicate this narrative. In the United States, you are legion!

After the German Revolution of 1848, these Turners and Acht-und-vierziger made America their adopted country and fought to preserve the Union in the American Civil War. As our story unfolds, you will rediscover them. Upon completion of reading the text, you will be committed to defend their good name, be guardian of their history, and emulate their virtues.

We, the authors, believe that you will wish to perpetrate those principles which they loved and you love also. You will desire to perpetuate their ideals, which made them glorious, and which you also cherish.

Copyright © 1988 by C. Eugene Miller

All rights reserved. Published in the United States of America. Calmar Publications, 202 Wildwood Lane, Louisville, Kentucky, 40223.

No parts of this book may be reproduced by any means, nor transmitted, nor translated into machine language without written permission of the publisher.

Printed in the United States of America at the University of Louisville, Louisville, Kentucky 40292.

Library of Congress Catalog Card Number: 88-70880
ISBN 0-9620368-0-3

The center of the village of Forchheim, Germany. Birthplace of Erhard Futterer. Prominent in the picture are the church and Ernst Fehr's home. Fehr has the collection of Futterer's letters. In 1987 Forchheim celebrated the 1225th anniversary of its founding. The village has a population of 981 and exists much as it was 156 years ago when Futterer was born.

ACKNOWLEDGEMENTS

One evening seventeen years ago, while rummaging through the forgotten contents of our attic, Marie, my wife, and I espied the portraits of her grandfather and grandmother, Erhard and Magdelena Futterer. They had been stored in our attic for 47 years and that evening we could not have imagined that Erhard Futterer would become the narrator of *Der Turner Soldat.* However, it has come to pass! The present treatise, describing the activities of the United Turner Rifles in the American Civil War, evolved out of a relentless but awkward genealogical safari through Erhard Futterer's life during the nineteenth century and a study of the Turner Movement in Europe and America. After the research was completed I concentrated my efforts on writing the text while Forrest Steinlage did the art work. Special attention should be given to his design of the dust cover.

It seems that the safari has been forever and has involved a long list of participants: authors, publishers, librarians, curators, relatives, friends, secretaries, historians, readers, financiers, and critics. The bibliography gives acknowledgement to authors and publishers. Librarians and curators of the following institutions are to be commended for their gracious help: University of Louisville, Louisville, Kentucky; University of Kentucky, Lexington, Kentucky; University of Vermont, Burlington, Vermont; Ann Mary Brown Memorial Library, Brown University, Providence, Rhode Island; New York City Public Library, New York City, New York; New York State Library, Albany, New York; Public Library, Troy, New York; Casemate Museum, Fortress Monroe, Virginia; Mariner's Museum, Newport News, Virginia; Public Library, Buffalo, New York; Generallandesarchiv, Karlsruhe, Baden, West Germany; and Buffalo Historical Society, Buffalo, New York. Finally, there are those who assisted graciously with their time and talents to bring the treatise to a publication. With no intention of listing them in the order of importance, but consolidating into categories, I proceed:

Relatives and Friends in Forchheim, West Germany: Ernst and Luise Fehr, relatives and curators of the Futterer letters, welcomed us into their home and shared with us the family genealogy; Hedwig Binder (deceased), retired village school teacher and author, gave us valuable insights into emigration from Forchheim in the 19th Century and conducted the villagers in translating the Futterer letters.

Relatives and Friends in America: Marie Ganey, Richard Rick, Marie M. Miller, Helen Siekmann, Arthur Futterer, Agnes Sippel, Eleanor Sibley (deceased), Edward Buchheit, Charles Buchheit and Richard Buchheit (deceased), grandchildren of Erhard Futterer, contributed their reminiscences; David Johnson, assistant director of the Casemate Museum, Fortress Monroe, Virginia, rendered valuable information and photographs of the 20th New York Regiment; Dr. Martin C. Striegel, Louisville, Kentucky offered historical documentation and letters of a veteran from the 5th New Hampshire Regiment, a veteran who was an eyewitness of the

Seven Days Battle of 1862. He also did the photography work to produce the pictures in the text; Edison Thomas, author and critic, Louisville, Kentucky, read the manuscript and suggested changes in the format of chapter one; Richard Bade, Fort Wayne, Indiana, discovered the source for the description of the uniforms worn by the 20th New York Regiment; Camille O'Leary, New York Military Museum, rendered her comments concerning the status of the United Turner Rifles' regimental flag; Benedict R. Maryniak, Buffalo Civil War Round Table, Buffalo, New York, helped us locate important source material in New York State; Hans H. Sammer, Theodore Dengler, and Frank Wedl, prominent members of the New York Turnverein, reviewed the unfinished manuscript and suggested changes which developed the treatise into a biographical narrative; Sister Clarita Felhoelter, retired English professor, Bellarmine College, Louisville, Kentucky, patiently reviewed and edited the completed manuscript.

Colleagues and Co-Workers at the University of Louisville, Louisville, Kentucky: Professor James Sutton, History Department, gave us valuable advice on 19th century European history and rendered criticism of the text; Professor Marta Edie, Modern Language Department, rendered advice on the proper usage of the German language in the text; Professor Jerry W. Cooney, History Department, gave a critical analysis of the Civil War chapters in the treatise; Professor Leon Fiedler, Department of Oral Surgery, interpreted the documentation of Erhard Futterer's wound at Antietam; Rose Marie Watters, LeAnne Whitney and Elissa V. Mills, Speed Scientific School, offered grammatical criticism; William Hawkins and Ernest Williams, Technicians, Electrical Engineering Department, assisted with computerized editing; Mark French and George Wilson, Speed Scientific School, helped with learning the operation of the microcomputer; Robert Vermillion, Technician, Civil Engineering Department, shared with us his knowledge and insights on Civil War armaments and uniforms.

Printers in Louisville, Kentucky: Mr. John Wilson, Grieb Printing Company, instructed us in the methods of desk top printing; Mr. Cliff Reid, Director of the University of Louisville's Print Shop, organized the printing of the text; Art Print Publishing Company and Welch Printing Company were generous of their time in offering commercial estimates of the cost of printing; Intercity Graphics explained the details of computerized typesetting.

To these and all others, who may have been inadvertently forgotten, my coauthor, Forrest Steinlage, and I offer our sincerest thanks!

C. Eugene Miller Ph.D.

PREFACE

In 1987, many moviegoers had the opportunity to see two spectacular films, *The Mission* and *Platoon*. Each deals with a serious subject matter in an historical setting. The setting of *The Mission* is unfamiliar to us, and few encyclopedia offer us enlightenment about its subject matter. *Platoon*, whose setting is the Vietnam War, has subject matter long faded from the six o'clock news. However, both these films captivated their audiences; it was easy to relate to them. They stress the human conflict in their respective historic settings! As such, both were tremendous box office successes.

C. Eugene Miller and Forrest Steinlage felt that the participation of the members of the New York Turnverein in the American Civil War would elicit the same kind of interest as these two films. Here, also, is a story of human conflict! When President Abraham Lincoln called for 75,000 volunteers on April 15, 1861, the Turnverein in New York responded immediately, formed a regiment, and served the Union for two years.

The New York Turnverein, founded in 1850, is a chapter of the physical education organization known as Turners, which has flourished in Europe and America, since being founded by Friedrich Ludwig Jahn in 1811, at Berlin, Germany. Turner is the German word for gymnast. In the United States, the national organization is known as the American Turners and their national headquarters is located in Louisville, Kentucky. Since the national organization's beginning, when ambitious and inspired young men, imbued with the spirit of progress and freedom, transplanted the ideals of Jahn to American soil, this organization has cleared its own path and has never lost sight of its ultimate goal: a sound mind in a sound body. Initially, it was German. Today, its membership is not limited to any one group of ethnic origin. However, two German expressions, Bahn Frei and Gut Heil, are still in colloquial use in the society. Bahn Frei is a Turner's expression, made just prior to a great race, Clear the Track. The other expression is an emotionally supportive, cheerful greeting of one athlete to another, Good Luck. These two expressions are featured in the present narrative concerning the activities of the 20th New York Regiment, which was formed by the New York Turnverein in answer to Lincoln's call to arms.

All the members of the 20th New York Regiment, the United Turner Rifles, were Turners and immigrants. Many had spent only a few years in America before the Civil War. They were Germans who spoke no English, or very little of it; but, surprisingly, had a devotion to the spirit of freedom and democracy which could match any native Americans'. Many were also Acht-und-vierziger, those who fled Germany, their fatherland, when the revolutionary movement there in 1848-1849 was supressed. Acht-und-vierziger means the '48ers. They were political refugees who came to America in order to escape persecution and the blight of reaction. They were an ethnic group trying to find, for the first time, their way in an adopted country, where discrimination easily resulted in fist fighting, rock throwing, and shooting.

Why did these Turners and Acht-und-vierziger fight in the Civil War, America's bloodiest war? Was their participation filled only with heroics and glamour, or was it a very human story? Steinlage and Miller felt they should attempt to answer these questions with a construction of the 20th New York Regiment's history, since neither the veterans of the regiment nor members of the various participating Turnvereine ever composed a detailed account of their activities in the war. Steinlage and Miller scheduled the publication of their narrative to coincide with the 125th anniversary of the Civil War.

The present work was originally envisioned as a genealogical study of Erhard Futterer, the grandfather of Miller's wife. Futterer emigrated from Baden in 1855, served as a private in Company B of the 20th New York Regiment, and was critically, but not mortally, wounded at Antietam on September 17, 1862. During his apprenticeship in Europe he was, for the first time, associated with the Turners, and his decision to emigrate was influenced by fellow athletes who had preceded him to America, subsequent to the German Revolution of 1848. During his apprenticeship in Freiburg, Germany, Futterer was also acquainted with several Acht-und-vierziger who subsequently participated in the American Civil War.

Miller collaborated with Steinlage, the national historian of the American Turners, who supplied Miller with a vast amount of source material on the Turner organizations in Europe and America. By combining their efforts, they were able to construct the regimental history, with an insight and appreciation for the education, wholesomeness, pride, courage, and frailty of the enlisted men and officers. The story which they relate is told in the first person. They allow Erhard Futterer to be der Turner Soldat (The Turner Soldier), who describes events and situations as Johnny Reb and Billy Yank do in Bell Irvin Wiley's Civil War classics.

Steinlage and Miller are not historians by profession. Steinlage is a retired engineer of the Metropolitan Sewer District, Louisville, Kentucky, and Miller is a professor of engineering mechanics at the University of Louisville. However, one could say humorously: "Their professions fit the present task; they know how to dig up the facts and put them together."

In the first three chapters, Futterer tells his story. He gives a reasonably accurate but, admittedly, incomplete military history of the 20th New York Regiment. He details the activities of the members of Company B, his company in the regiment. From his story, we learn that the Turners, who volunteered for service in the Civil War, were pure and idealistic but subject to human frailty. They were ordinary men doing ordinary things in an extraordinary manner; as such, they achieved greatness. At the end of his story, Futterer challenges the organization of American Turners; he encourages its membership to produce a scholarly history of the regiment.

Miller extends the treatise by adding a chapter, in which he shows how, through combining bits and pieces of scattered information, the story, as told by Futterer, was developed.

The authors believe they have presented, with illustrations, a story never before told; one that will hold the readers' interest and make Turners proud of their beginning in America. The work should also have appeal to a much broader audience. Recently, we celebrated the anniversary of the German minority's immigrating to America. It was said, on that occasion, "At least 60 million Americans carry a German name." These should find the narrative fascinating, since, for so long a time, the German contribution in the Civil War has not been emphasized in popular literature. Finally, the authors believe that the narration should have appeal to Vietnam War veterans. Several of the human elements in the story parallel those experienced by these veterans: fear associated with combat near the end of one's service period, poor leadership resulting in excessive and unnecessary casualties, and failure to receive appreciation for one's service upon muster-out while the war lingers on.

C. Eugene Miller Ph.D
Forrest Steinlage L.S.
Louisville, Kentucky
September 17, 1987

TABLE OF CONTENTS

DER TURNER SOLDAT 13

THE FIRST YEAR OF WAR 43

THE SOLDIERS WE WERE TRAINED TO BE 73

THE PRIVATE'S CHALLENGE 103

THE AUTHORS' APOLOGIA 105

FROM BITS AND PIECES 107

BIBLIOGRAPHY 115

DER TURNER SOLDAT

My name is Erhard Futterer. One hundred and twenty-five years ago, I was a private in Company B, the 20th New York Volunteers, the United Turner Rifles. My regiment, composed of 1,200 members of several Turnvereine in the East, but recruited mainly from the environs of New York City, fought for two years on the side of the Union in the American Civil War.

Many American writers have created a clear picture of the social history which influenced and motivated the nativistic Union and Confederate soldiers. However, they did not give the same attention to the German immigrants who also served as enlisted men in the armies of both the North and the South. Some German authors have given many statistics concerning the numerous German regiments which fought in the Civil War and have related biographies of ranking officers in these regiments. However, these authors fell short in giving insight that developed appreciation for the education, wholesomeness, pride, and courage of the German enlisted man. Unfortunately, very little has been written about him. Why did he emigrate from Europe to America? Why did he associate with the American Turner Movement? Why did the various Turnvereine in America form regiments out of their membership? Why did the Turners volunteer to fight in the American Civil War?

Although the Turner movement in America was inaugurated in 1848 and Turnvereine had proliferated throughout the country by 1861, their members have not attempted to describe the social history of those who filled the ranks of Turner regiments. In order to compensate for this lack of knowledge and being a Turner both in Europe as well as in America, I was chosen to tell my origin, education, motivation for emigration, and romance with my adopted country. My origin, lifestyle, and career may not be typical of all 1,200 members of the Turnvereine in the environs of New York who joined the regiment, but they are not atypical either.

I was born on August 30, 1831, in the village of Forchheim in Baden, Germany. Today, it exists much as it was 156 years ago. It has a population of 981 and is situated adjacent to the Kaiserstuhl, 14 miles west of Freiburg. The area is known as Breisgau and lies between the Rhine River and the Black Forest in southwestern Germany. The church, the Rathaus (town hall), the layout of the streets, and the home in which I was born remain as they were when I left the village to come to America in 1855. During the nineteenth century, 526 people from 42 families emigrated from Forchheim and its environs to the Americas. Amongst them are the families of: Eckert, Futterer, Gerber, Haberstroh, Weiman, Weis, Grimm, Loesch, Stiehl, Schwarzle, Binder, Dienst, Bettinger, Haas, Benzinger, Fendrich, Hildebrand, Keck, Kuhn, Mast, and Ries.

I credit my grandmother, Magdelena Ziebold Futterer, as being my very first teacher. During the winter months, my sisters, Theresa and Francesca, and I would gather around her and revel in listening to her relate stories of German folklore and our lineage. We learned how our ancestors, who had originally occupied themselves as animal caretakers, had been persecuted by the Calvinists in Switzerland during the Thirty Years War, fled the country, and found refuge in Forchheim.

Often she spoke of my grandfather, Martin Futterer, and his family. Martin was born in 1766. His parents died in 1788 just before he married my grandmother. His uncles — Andreas, Johann, Jacob, and Joseph — had emigrated from our village to Hungary. Andreas, the eldest, left Forchheim in 1752; and Joseph, the youngest, departed in 1764. They had received land grants from Francis I, Archduke of Austria and Emperor of the Holy Roman Empire. At that time, Baden was a faithful satellite of Austria, and Archduke Francis I was desirous of having those of German blood and language settle in Hungary, be the leading class there, and have a political impact upon the country. Francis died in 1765 but his wife, Maria Theresa, ruled Austria, Hungary, and Bohemia until her death in 1780. She continued to honor all the land grants given to the Germans by her husband. My parents' devotion to the memory of these two great rulers was exemplified in their giving the names of Theresa and Francesca to their daughters. Grandma liked to remind us that she influenced my parents in their decision.

Grandma told us about her early married life. When Martin married Magdelena, he was 22 years old and she 17. They looked for a bright and prosperous future and accepted the invitation of Martin's uncles to make Hungary their home. The uncles sent money for Martin's and Magdelena's travel expenses and offered them a share in their Hungarian land holdings provided Martin would cultivate the holdings and be of assistance in local politics. After Martin and Magdelena had been in Hungary for a time, they began to dislike their surroundings. The country appeared to be an outpost of civilization in which the people constantly feared an invasion from the Turks. Magdelena especially felt much alone and longed for her relatives and friends in Baden. In 1794, Martin and Magdelena extended their gratitude to the uncles but insisted that they could stay no longer. They returned to Forchheim where my father, Joseph, was born in 1801.

Upon returning, they found the Breisgau valley very peaceful. Austria had completed her war with France. The King of France, Louis XVI, had been deposed and the reign of terror following the French Revolution was coming to a halt. Peace did not last! The military and political activities of the French again created an atmosphere which sent discouraging and fearful winds toward Baden and the Palatinate, the German State north of Baden.

In 1804, the French Republic was declared an Empire, and Napoleon Bonaparte took the title of emperor. Napoleon cunningly absorbed the small kingdoms of Germany into his empire and raised the electoral princes to the rank of king. Baden had been united in 1771 by Karl Frederick; but, in 1807, following the demise of the Holy Roman Empire and with the encouragement of Bonaparte, Frederick formed it into a Grand Duchy and entered it into the Confederation of the Rhine. He married the French noble lady, Stephanie de Beauharnais. She was Napoleon's adopted daughter. As a consequence of these political and romantic alliances, Baden was subsequently drawn into the wars of the French Empire.

Having political ambitions, my grandfather, Martin, joined the French army and fought in several battles which Napoleon had with the Austrians in 1809. At the end of the Austrian campaign, Martin returned to Forchheim and Karl Frederick rewarded him by appointing him the Vogte of our village in 1811. He held this title of administrator until 1826. In 1844, the title was changed to Buergermeister, which is village mayor.

After the defeat of Napoleon by the Great Alliance of Prussia, Russia, Austria, and Great Britain, Karl Frederick continued to hold power in Baden. He placed the state in the German Confederation and allowed a liberal constitution to be established in 1818. Property owners began to pay taxes in the amount of property owned without regard to social status. The method of tax collection became more efficient. Church courts were abolished and persons of all religions received the same civil rights. In essence, a new system of local government replaced the quaint peculiarities of old fashioned towns.

In Forchheim, Martin, now the Vogte, instructed his people about the benefits of being associated with the German Confederation, the concessions and restrictions of the new constitution, and the need for justifiable taxation. Karl Frederick died in 1830 and was succeeded by Leopold, who was called the Volksfreund, that is, friend of the people. His reputation of being beloved did not last long since he was not very liberal in the application of Karl Frederick's liberal constitution. By this time, Stefan Loesch had succeeded Martin as Vogte but Martin used his influence to fight against Leopold's unjust methods of applying parity in crop growth and distribution. He also publicly spoke out against Leopold's plan of limiting private ownership of land and initiating unjust taxation. It is quite understandable why Leopold did not shed tears when my grandfather died in 1832. However, Magdelena survived Martin and continued to be a source of wisdom to our family until her death in 1846.

In 1837, I began my formal education at the local village school called the Volksschule. Each village and town in Baden had one, supported by the taxes collected by the Duke. Those who attended the Volksschule on Baerenstrasse in Forchheim received a respectable education. They learned to read, write, and do mathematics adequately. A graduate of the Volksschule who had no desires for higher learning made a good producer, a good farmer, a good soldier, and a docile respecter of the Duke and his laws. However, if he did not seek some kind of additional training, he could not enter the professions or be employed in the crafts or skilled trades which offered a better financial reward in life. So, when I graduated from the Volksschule at the age of 15, my father and I discussed alternatives for my future education.

The Gymnasium was a high school, par excellence. At the time I was of age to attend, one needed the state committee's approval for admission and only if I attended the Gymnasium could I be accepted into the university. However, my father told me that he could not obtain for me the state committee's approval. So, we discussed the possibility of attending some other type of high school. We knew that the old Latin schools, where originally all courses were taught in the Latin language, had become Buerger Schools, Town Schools, or Realschule. Now, courses were taught in these schools in German and young people were educated for clerical and technical avocations, and their graduates obtained positions in commerce and industry without attending the university. Possibly, I might have obtained a good education in one of these schools even though the teachers were not accepted as equals to those in the Gymnasium. However, the Realschule was not held in high esteem by the clergy of the Church. The pastor of our village warned my parents that the Realschule, in Freiburg, was the breeding ground of materialism, irregularity, and revolution. He said, "The teachers advocate a change in society, lack respect for authority, raise the knowledge of useful things above faith, and belittle the rewards of common toil in the fields." I did not consider our pastor to be of intellectual ilk. He could not accept most deeds and ideas that were progressive. It was always easier for him to hide from reality by living in the confines of faith alone. My parents were staunch Catholics and blindly agreed with him. They were also devoted farmers. Hence I, to please them, had to be obedient to their wishes. I also agreed openly with my pastor.

So, even though I was growing up in an era when a class of people was emerging who owed their status to educational qualifications rather than hereditary rights and needed no great capital or large land holdings to be considered superior, I was being stifled by my family's clinging to the status quo. I was just a farmer's son unable to begin to share in the opportunities of the sons of lawyers, ministers, and government officials. Although I realized my limited opportunities, I still insisted that there must be a better way, a more exciting way, to make a living than being a farmer. I felt that I had one last alternative. I could seek an education in the crafts as an apprentice. However, before I could make a choice of what craft I would enjoy most, I had to take inventory of my own talents and abilities.

Fortunately, while at the Volksschule, I came under the influence of Franz Kuhn who gave me an enthusiasm for fresco painting, goldleafing, and interior decorating. He was unique, loved teaching, and had an insatiable appetite to share himself and his talents with his students. He must have been a very secure person because in giving of himself he never seemed to fear that he was being drained in that giving. One would also think that his knowledge was infinite because he never gave the impression that there was an end to what he was imparting to others. He was friendly with many mastercraftsmen in Breisgau, especially Ludwig Junginger in Freiburg. It was through Kuhn that I received an introduction to Junginger and discussed the possibility of my doing an apprenticeship with him.

Before I made a final decision to accept the apprenticeship, I made a serious attempt to learn as much as I could concerning the various trades available to a young person. Some of the best salaried jobs were held by woodcutters in the Schwarzwald, the Black Forest. They made $240 per year, denied themselves nothing, and constantly ate meat and drank the best wine. They had secure and steady work and were traditionally unmarried men with no families. I was not attracted to their style of life.

Above all, I knew I did not wish to be a farmer. On the farms much greater than my parents had, the hired laborers and servants received their board and were given about $25 per year in wages. In the morning they would eat soup, potatoes, and bread. For dinner they would have bread, potatoes, and soup. In cold weather they might partake of some inferior brandy before going out into the fields in the afternoon. Only on Sunday could they afford to have beer or allow their women to drink coffee. This kind of life seemed to me to be very austere and to lack any hope of a bright future.

Upon further investigation, I found that the best paid factory workers in Germany were associated with the dye industry. They received about $200 per year. In the trades, printers, brewers, bakers, gilders, cabinetmakers, watchmakers, and pastry cooks led the best paid list with about $350 per year. Gunsmiths, jewelers, carvers, nailers, goldsmiths, papermakers, locksmiths, stonecutters, tailors, and tanners held second place with an annual income of $290 per year. The average wage earners among the craftsmen were the toymen, capmakers, hatters, shoemakers, carpenters, cartwrights, cutters, tinmen, masons, perfumers, paviors, plumbers, coachmakers, upholsterers, coopers, and blacksmiths. They could expect an annual wage of $150 for their efforts. Some laborers were offered board and room along with their wages. Butchers, brewers, and pastry cooks were usually employed in this manner.

In the end, I decided to take the apprenticeship with Junginger in Freiburg. He had as many as 20 young men working for him at one time. Late in the year 1848, I moved into his apprenticeship dormitories and began my work and studies; I made acquaintances. I met members of the university fraternity called Burschen. They frequented a tavern-like establishment called a Kneipe, let their hair grow extremely long, wore velvet coats, and smoked tobacco from long, ornate pipes. They had received the reputation of being drinkers and card players in the hours when they were not studying. The ruling class of Baden was disdainful of them and objected to their liberal mentality and their seeming disrespect for authority.

I was also introduced to the Turners; their founder, Friedrich Ludwig Jahn, had just recently at the age of 70 made his home in Freiburg, and he occasionally attended our meetings. He had founded the Turners in 1811 while he was a teacher in Berlin; and, for 37 years, he had been held in high esteem as Turnvater Jahn. Although in his later life his influence over many young Germans decreased, I felt that it was a great privilege to know him personally; he had done so much in strengthening and liberalizing German youth. He liked to say, "The education of the people aims to realize the ideal of an all- around human being, citizen, and member of society in each individual; gymnastics are one means toward a complete education of the people." He founded the gymnastic Turners based on the Greek system first proposed in Germany by Johann GuthMuths in 1793. However, Jahn's program also instilled into his young gymnasts a spirit of liberalism, democracy, and pride in being German. His programs were condemned by Metternich and the Karlsbad Decrees in 1819. The interdict was not lifted until 1842. At that time the groups which had lived underground began to flourish with increased membership throughout all the German states and kingdoms. The Turner slogan was, "Frisch, fromm, froeh, frei" (bold, devout, happy, free). Often I heard the Turners chant,

>Freedom is a diamond pure,
>Not glass to break and shatter.
>Though oft the folk with hand unsure
>May let it drop — what matter?

I was most attracted to them and well impressed as I saw their display of a free spirit. I could not help but be brought to a high pitch of emotion when I heard them voice the words of the Roman author Juvenal, "Mens sana in corpore sano," which means "A sound mind in a sound body."

During my Lehrjahre, my years of apprenticeship, revolution broke out in the German states. The years 1848 and 1849 were difficult ones for the Badener. Revolutionary troops roamed the countryside pursued by the royal guards. For a time, the city of Freiburg was under siege. Throughout all the German states there was unrest in the towns and villages. The Frankfurt Parliament was convened by the intellectuals of the land. Even Jahn for a short time joined this august body. There were high hopes that a unification of the German states could be achieved and a constitutional government could be established. Although the smaller German states were represented, the strong influence of Prussia and Austria, where the wealth and power rested, seemed to predominate in opposition to the liberals. The revolution was so important to us, but there seemed to be little knowledge of it in the outside world. Only the President of the United States, James Polk, sent a message of encouragement and congratulation to the Frankfurt Parliament.

Baden, Wuerttemburg, and the Palatinate were exposed to patches of serious armed conflict between the armies of the Grand Duke and the ill-equipped bands led by liberals such as Sigel, Hecker, and Struve. For a short time, these latter were successful on the small battlefields. It was a strange kind of war. There were no clear and well-defined lines of battle. It was mainly a civil upheaval in which the liberals tried to excite the populace to rise in protest against a despotic form of government led by Leopold. For all their disorganization, they were able to bring about his temporary abdication, during which he fled the country. However, he called upon the Prussians to intervene, and they responded by sending their army into Baden. The revolutionaries thought they could outwit the Prussians, make the towns and villages pockets of resistance, and play for time until some form of constitutional law could be established. However, the Frankfurt Parliament failed to achieve its goal, and it was dissolved. None of the leading princes of Prussia or Austria wished to accept the challenge to promote such a radical change as constitutional government. They were willing to make some small concessions to alleviate the rigors of life for the working class, but they were totally averse to government by the people, and they were absolutely opposed to granting the universal right to vote.

Through this confused period, I continued with my apprenticeship in Freiburg. I was never directly exposed to the violence except for the period when the city was under siege. During that time, I met Adolf Dengler, one of the revolutionary officers, who was defending the city. He was a capmaker and most of the apprentices had made purchases at his shop. After the revolution failed, he fled by way of Switzerland to America and settled in Belleville, Illinois. During the American Civil War, he joined the Union Army and was killed at Vicksburg on May 22, 1863.

Our food was scarce and needless to say there were no luxuries. Junginger kept us working at our trade and warned us to keep a neutral mentality toward the revolutionaries and royalists. On one occasion he said, "I do not mind that you are friendly with Dengler but do not offer him any assistance; especially do not carry messages for him." It was good that we did not do so. By the end of 1849, the Prussians dominated in the towns and villages, subdued the bands of militants, and established order. As the winter of 1850 turned to spring, all could see that the revolution was a complete failure. The militant leaders had either fled the country or were imprisoned. Many of them were my neighbors from the towns and villages around Forchheim.

One of those neighbors was Gustav Wilhelm Eisenlohr. He had been born in Loerrach and studied theology at Halle and Heidelberg. For a period of time, he was pastor in Emmendingen, a town six kilometers east of Forchheim. As a refugee in America, he was a pastor at New Braunfels, Texas and in Cincinnati, Ohio. Carl Kiefer from Emmendingen was also forced to leave his home because of his activities in the revolution. He settled in Philadelphia in 1849 and was a good friend of my sister's husband, George Zell. Wilhelm Rothacker, another militant, fled with Dengler and died a natural death in America at the age of 31. Constantin Rosswog, a goldsmith from Endingen, another town four kilometers from my village, took part in the Freiburg defense and later emigrated to New York City with his wife and children. He was active in the American Turner Movement and was one of the 36 original founders of the New York Socialistischer Turnverein in 1850. From my own village, Johann Dienst was forced to flee Baden. He died of wounds he received on the battlefield of Antietam on September 17, 1862. All Germans such as these were later known in America as the Acht-und-vierziger because they had been associated with the German Revolution of 1848.

Those who left the fatherland, after the revolution, were sadly missed by their friends and relatives whom they left behind, but they were heartily greeted by new friends in their adopted countries. There was no lack of intellectualism among those who sought and fought for freedom in 1848-1849 in our state of Baden. The ranks of the insurgents were filled with journalists, physicians, teachers, businessmen, authors, diplomats, musicians, engineers, pastors, and poets. The same spirit of liberalism equally touched those who were farmers, artisans, craftsmen, and innkeepers. Most of them were very young, in their early and mid twenties. When the conflict was over, they left the fatherland out of necessity but they did not hate it. Often they were heard to sing,

>Kein Baum gehoerte mir von deinen Waeldern,
>Mein war kein Halm auf deinen Roggenfeldern,
>Und schutzlos hast du mich hinausgetrieben,
>Weil ich in meiner Jugend nicht verstand
>Dich weniger und mehr mich selbst zu lieben,
>Und dennoch lieb ich dich, mein Vaterland!

In translating into English a German poem I find that much of the real feeling is lost, but I will attempt to express the feeling of these Acht-und-vierziger as best I can.

>In all the forests was no tree my own;
>No blade of rye in all thy fields was mine;
>Thou cast me out defenseless and alone,
>So young and simple I could not divine
>That I should love thee less, myself the more;
>Still, fatherland, I love thee as before!

The revolution had ended in bitter disappointment and disillusionment. However, it stirred up everything that was alive in the state, in society, and in the church whether old or new in origin. It somehow gave light and room for everything to unfold in keeping with its innate strength. The freedom to do something awakens the desire to do it. For one brief moment, all tasted freedom and the taste was good especially to the young. I could not help but be touched and inspired by it all.

However, my life went on. Just before Christmas in 1851, my Lehrjahre came to an end and I returned home for the holidays. I considered myself no longer a youth. I was a man at the age of 20. Arriving at home, I discovered that the preceding year had been a poor one at the farm. The potato rot had infested the land. My father planted only one-third of his tillable soil; and, even though he substituted turnips for potatoes, he had little success that year. In the winter months, a farmer usually rests quietly thanking God for the season's harvest and planning for a better season in the spring. That Christmas, an unsuccessful harvest placed an ominous pall over the entire family.

During those holidays, I discussed with my parents the next step in the pursuit of my career. When the snows would depart in the spring I would be leaving Forchheim for the capital, Karlsruhe. There, I would make all the arrangements for my Wanderjahre, which meant my years working as an apprentice journeyman. This would be the second step in the long process of completing the work required to obtain my master-craftsman's license as a fresco painter, gilder, and interior decorator. This announcement added to the family sadness because once again I would be leaving home for an extended period of time.

Probably my decision to leave home again was a wise one. In my conversations with my parents during those Christmas holidays I could see that they and I were politically and philosophically moving further apart. They still held fast to the status quo, while I was generating within myself strong feelings of liberalism, forceful expressions for freedom, and dissatisfaction with the traditional way of life to which they had become accustomed. As we looked at our German flag called the Tricolors (black, red, and gold), they and I saw a different symbolism. In those colors, they saw themselves as devoted, obedient members of what I considered a fading paternalistic society. For me they symbolized coming out of the black night of slavery, being soaked in the bloody strife of the revolution, and going into the golden dawn of freedom.

> Black, Red and Gold, these are the colors
> We Germans proudly bear on high;
> Black, Red and Gold, these are the colors
> For which we fight and gladly die.
>
> The Black betokens death to tyrants
> Who laughingly nailed us to a tree;
> And Red's the blood we poured as offering
> For Justice and Liberty.
>
> But Gold is freedom blossoming
> That men, their duty done, may see;
> so fly on highways and on by ways
> The sacred German colors three.

Since I did not actively participate in the revolution, I could not truly consider myself an Acht-und-vierziger. However, I knew that I was so influenced by it that I was completely molded in the spirit of '48. It was with this spirit that I crossed over from youth to manhood. I was optimistic and filled with enthusiasm. Now my success would depend upon my opportunity to apply the knowledge I had learned as an apprentice while at the same time receiving an adequate remuneration for my efforts. In the German states, the method whereby I was to enter the workforce and procure an acceptable wage was complicated.

In 1819 an intergovernmental organization known as the Zollverein was created in central Europe by the 39 autonomous German states. It was a custom union which determined economic and trade policies for the individual states with their mutual cooperation and input. Under strict regulation, the Zollverein allowed labor migration, proposed a minimum but fluctuating wage scale, and permitted work to be performed in all towns and villages by the Auslaender as well as the resident. The Auslaender was a transient worker who prior to the establishment of the Zollverein was unable to procure work in a village other than his own. The Innung, the local union of each village, had established this policy.

By 1852, it appeared that this practice, a remnant of the old guild system, had been abolished. However, the allocation of work assignments was still directed by the local mastercraftsman, and it was illegal, even under the Zollverein policy, to contract work in his village unless he approved. Also, the mastercraftsman could require the Auslaender to apply for work only within the confines of a strict definition of the Auslaender's craft or trade. Further, the Zollverein policy only required the mastercraftsman to give the Auslaender work when such work was in excess of what the members of the Innung could perform. The mastercraftsman's judgment in this regard was final, and the Auslaender had no right of appeal. These practices presented the Auslaender with a most distressing dilemma. If he did not obtain a mastercraftsman license, he could look forward to being forever a traveling, starving, and sporadically employed journeyman. However, he could not obtain the license until he had proven his skill through job performance.

Fortunately, the Zollverein introduced the Wanderschaft system. Through it, an apprentice who had completed his Lehrjahre could obtain his license by spending a certain number of years practicing his avocation outside his native locale. He would follow a planned itinerant progam which was probationary. It was called his Wanderjahre. The Wanderschaft system had the blessing of the licensed craftsmen. To them it presented no threat. To them it was considered educational. They also had no commitment of permanent employment of the apprentice journeyman who was on his Wanderjahre. The licensed craftsmen were also provided with cheap labor for whatever period they desired. I do not know the origin of this peculiarity in the supply of labor in the crafts and trades but, in 1852, it was the rule in Switzerland, Austria, and Germany. I can only surmise that it was there as the result of immemorial usage, and many young apprentices seized the opportunity to participate in order to avoid the plight of the Auslaender.

When I completed my apprenticeship with Junginger in Freiburg, I desired to reach the epitome of my career as a fresco painter, gilder, and decorator. On March 7, 1852, I went by rail to Karlsruhe, the capital of Baden, where I embarked upon my internship in the Wanderschaft. I spent five days in the capital preparing with the state authorities my Wanderjahre itinerary. First, I registered at the Departments of Interior and Travel. I presented them with my name, date and place of birth, and a definition of my profession. They compiled a complete physical description of me making short but pertinent comments concerning my stature, face, hair, forehead, eyebrows, eyes, nose, mouth, teeth, chin, beard, and any distinguishing disfigurations. I was a short lad, five feet and four inches in height with blond hair and eyebrows, blue eyes, and a high forehead. They filed this description at the ministries and recorded it in a Wanderbuch which they presented to me.

This booklet was composed of 32 pages with 64 usable sides. Page one contained the control stamp and seal of the state of Baden along with an issue number. Page two was reserved for all pertinent comments concerning my physical condition, and space was reserved for remarks about my conduct. If I had any former criminal record, which fortunately I did not, it would have been recorded. Also, I was most thankful that I had remained neutral during the revolution, as suggested by Junginger, because any insurgent activity would have been recorded. Page three contained my complete physical description and my signature. Page four contained a statement directed to the authorities in the 39 German states, both civil and military. It read, "The signer and carrier of this Wanderbuch, Erhard Futterer, is on his Wanderjahre; and, as long as he performs his duties under the rules of the Department of the Interior and Travel conforming to the policy of the Wanderschaft, he is exempt from military service and is to receive all the rights and privileges afforded this contract." Attached to this statement was the seal of the Baden Ministry of Interior and Travel. This statement was dated March 7, 1852. Pages five to ten contained the rules and regulations which I was to follow, and the remaining pages were left blank. These were to be completed by the police and the mastercraftsmen in the cities, towns, and villages which I was approved to visit.

These rules were first written in 1824 and revised in 1841. At the end of the book, both in German and Flemish, a set of punishments were listed for infractions.

My wages were set at $1 per week, if and when I could find work. One of the privileges provided to the apprentice journeyman was his right to legally beg. I was not expected to survive on my given wage, but I was allowed, with the approval of the police, to ask for charitable donations to assist me in my physical support. Before making my request to a prospective benefactor, I would show him my Wanderbuch. Then, I would inform him of my needs. If I received a favorable response, I would spend some time with him in conversation. In this way, I felt like a newscaster, discussing events and working conditions in the towns and villages I had visited. Many benefactors looked forward to hearing about wages offered by the various trades and crafts in other parts of Europe. This kind of information was of special interest to the foreign travelers I accosted, but some of them showed outright disgust for the policy of begging.

On one occasion, I met a Scotsman who feared that legalized begging removed for me the reluctance to continue so degrading a resource in life after my internship was over. He was convinced that I would continue the policy when stress might arise, and then I would not have the extenuating circumstance which custom was now affording me. He further shared with me his suspicion that I might be practicing the fine art of vagabondizing. I tried to convince him that most of the apprentices were truly in need of support but that I did know of some interns who had had their Wanderbuch stolen and used falsely by professional vagabonds.

After I received my Wanderbuch, the ministries gave me a full plan for my itinerary. It contained a list of towns and villages which I was to visit and the names of the mastercraftsmen in each with whom I was to seek employment. Upon my completion of any work with them, they were to sign, stamp, and affix their license number to my book. They would also write a short comment of praise or disatisfaction. This was equivalent to receiving grades in a modern school, and a fully annotated Wanderbuch was the same as a diploma. Only through this system could I fulfill the requirements necessary to receive my license, which would allow me to be recognized as a mastercraftsman, solicit my own work projects, and subsequently employ my own young apprentices.

On my Wanderjahre, I studied under masters outside Freiburg, painting frescoes, gilding, and decorating walls and ceilings. Some masters were not as talented as their apprentices, but the Wanderjahrer showed the craftsman great respect. The apprentice journeyman honored the master's experience and position. A few old masters went so far as to give up their practices to the young interns upon completion of the latter's Wanderjahre. These old craftsmen took pride in passing on their talents to posterity through those young men to whom they voluntarily chose to surrender their practice. However, all masters graciously shared their ideas and techniques with the apprentice journeyman. This seemed to be innate to their profession. On my Wanderjahre I was most grateful to all the craftsmen I worked with. I truly grew in experience and added materially to my knowledge and mental capacity. The Scotsman who had denounced the practice of begging confided to me that all the interns he had met on the continent far surpassed the same class of beginners in his homeland. He was especially impressed by the young German's maturity in general education. Proudly, I suggested to him that my village Volksschule was mainly responsible for my maturity.

The Wanderschaft system was highly structured. On entering a town I was required to present myself to the local police and present them with my Wanderbuch. They recorded the date and time of my arrival, checked the name of the mastercraftsman I was to see, and verified the signature, seal, and license number of the craftsman in the village I had come from. Only then was I allowed to proceed on my way. From the time of my initial registration, I was given 24 hours to make contact with the master I came to seek employment with; and, if I were unable to make contact, I was to return to the police. I had to tell them where I was staying overnight; and, if they approved, I was awarded a second day of grace to try again.

Each village had a Herberge, a designated inn where the Innung reserved space at a very low rate for the Wanderjahrer. Whenever I came to a village, I would request immediately the name and location of the Gilders Herberge and stay there for the first night. However, after I found employment I made other arrangements. Quickly, I learned to depend on charity. Although the fee at the Herberge was very small, it was much better to find lodging at a place that was free. In most villages and towns, the residents were very gracious in providing free accommodations once I had obtained work.

At no time was I allowed to stray further than a three-mile radius from police headquarters without the companionship of local fellow workers. For infraction of this or any of the other rules, I would be sentenced from one to three days in the local prison, where I would be required to subsist only on bits of bread and rations of water. Each infraction would be recorded in my Wanderbuch and, if it were repeated, I would be sentenced to eight days in prison, during which time the bread bits would become smaller and the water ration more "rationed."

Before leaving Karlsruhe, I was informed of one alternative. If, in a certain city, I found work which was subsequently terminated, I was allowed to go on with my itinerary and return to that city if I had been promised a future assignment there at the time of my termination. Also, I was ordered to write a progress report periodically to the office of the Ministry of the Interior and Travel; and, every three months, I had to inform my parents by letter of my whereabouts. The letter had to contain a description of my work.

I was warned that it was extremely important for me to keep my Wanderbuch in a safe place, preferably on my person. If I lost it, I was to immediately report the loss to the local police. It was a thoroughly annoying procedure, but the book could be replaced at a cost of 36 kreuzer, approximately 18 cents, a day's wage. However, the accrued masters' signatures and comments could never be replaced.

On March 12, 1852, I completed the required preparations at the capital. I returned to Forchheim, showed my parents the plan, and informed them that I would be starting my Wanderjahre immediately. I planned to travel by rail as much as possible. The first German overland system was completed in 1827, connecting the cities of Nuremberg and Fuerth. Subsequently, rail systems proliferated and were conveniently interconnected. The stage roads had also been improved and water travel was excellent but slow.

On March 15, I set out for my first assignment in the city of Heidelberg. For the first time, I went through the rituals of registering, finding lodging, and reporting to the mastercraftsman. On March 17, he accepted me and I was given my first job assignment. At the Ochsen, a small inn near the river, I painted ornate flower designs on the walls. The next month, our work crews began painting in other buildings, but I was told that my services were no longer needed. I felt the pang of dismissal. On April 19, I received a favorable evaluation from the master and received my wages.

A group of Burschen took pity on me and offered me some money which I used to pay for my board at the Herberge. While I stayed in Heidelberg, I had the privilege of seeing the great castle. On seeing it, I recalled the romantic stories Grandma Magdelena told me when I was a child. They were filled with unbelievable adventures of the aristocracy living in like castles along the Rhine River from Mainz to Cologne. The number of these castles and the number of stories about them were legion!

I could not tarry. I was on to Mannheim where no assignments were available; I could not believe it; Mannheim was so large. I had to accept the mastercraftsman's denial without explanation. I was not about to be obnoxious by questioning him. He stamped and signed my Wanderbuch but recorded that I did not work for him. Since I had no work, I received no pay. I needed passage money. Near the dock along the Neckar River in a park where red tulips were growing in neatly planted rows, I stopped several tourists; and, within an hour, I had begged enough money for my passage to Heilbronn; I arrived on April 22.

Work opportunities were not plentiful, but the mastercraftsman, being a kind and jovial man, allowed me to fulfill my requirement by putting me on one of his crews until May 6. I was involved with a redecoration of the Rathaus, and I was fortunate to find lodging at the home of the Buergermeister. The mayor's wife took a liking to me; and, after she had stuffed me with her Apfelstrudel, for which I graciously thanked and complimented her, she offered me the spare room which she had available. I immediately accepted the offer. Because of her generosity, I would be able to leave the village well fed, with my book signed, and having $2 saved.

On May 7, I went by rail to Ludwigsburg, arriving the next day. I was offered work that lasted until September 22. Immediately, I was placed on the fresco team that was doing art work on the ceiling of the bishop's private chapel. I learned a new painting process called the stirred-chromatic technique. It was first discovered by a chemist, Obergrath von Fuchs, who lived in Munich. I was shown how to mix my colors with water and, after completing a section of mural, how to sprinkle the whole scene with more water and a bit of fluoric acid as a mix. In this way, the painted scene became hardened quickly, and it could be retouched and glazed easily; a new experience; something I did not learn from Junginger in Freiburg.

While I was in Ludwigsburg, one of the apprentices was involved in a Gasthaus brawl. After being arrested at the tavern, he was confined in the local prison. It was his third offense and subsequent to his release his Wanderjahre was terminated. While he was in prison, I visited him and learned some interesting facts about the German penal system from the attending guards. Most of the men and women prisoners who were convicted for theft, assault, and prostitution were uneducated, whereas among the educated the major crime was fraud. In a survey taken in several German states, only 4 percent of those in jail were from the educated class. Also, while in prison, women were assigned manual work inside the jail, but males were used throughout the cities as street sweepers; this sentence was given deliberately to those convicted of fraud so they could experience public humiliation.

At the end of September, I left Ludwigsburg and continued my plan, going in order to Stuttgart, Ulm, and Gunzberg. In these cities, the masters signed my book but did not provide me with any work experience. On September 25, I arrived in Augsburg and worked there until December 12. While doing so, I was fortunate enough to board with an uncle of one of the local apprentices. I had written to my parents and told them where I was staying, and my parents offered to reciprocate with lodging if one of the apprentices in Augsburg went west to work out his Wanderjahre in Breisgau. While staying with the family of the apprentice's uncle, I learned how much it cost a man, his wife, and two children to live rather comfortably; all worked for a weekly wage. The uncle earned $2.25 as a plumber, and his wife received $1.50 as a weaver. Each of the children, who made deliveries for the local market, was paid $0.53. The uncle recorded the family's weekly expenditures, and the following is the budget he gave me. I found it so interesting that I sent it to my parents with my letter.

    Rent for the cottage for four $0.24
    Bread; 26 pounds 0.75
    Bacon; 8 pounds 0.90
    Coal; (used all year) 0.39
    Potatoes and vegetables; 1 bushel 0.30

Beer; 14 quarts	0.36
Tea and Coffee; (2 ounces = $0.75)	0.12
Sugar; ($0.10 per pound)	0.15
Butter;($0.19 per pound)	0.29
Cheese; 1 pound	0.14
Milk; 3 quarts	0.09
Soap; 1 pound	0.11
Candles; 1 pound	0.12
Tobacco; 1 ounce	0.05
Husband's clothing; (1 suit, 2 pair shoes per year)	0.24
Wife's clothing; (2 suits per year)	0.15
Children's clothing	0.24
Local Gasthaus	0.09
Recreation	0.09

I also learned that whatever these people could save they put away toward the purchase of a house, but achieving that goal was a dream. A four-room cottage cost approximately $600 with a down payment of $100 and a mortgage on the borrowed remainder levied at an annual interest rate of 5 percent.

From Augsburg, I went to Munich, the capital and principal city of Bavaria and the home of King Ludwig, the Art King. Situated on the edge of the German Alps, it held in aesthetical honor the edelweiss, the white flower that bloomed in the snow along the mountain slopes. As I entered the city, I could see art and beauty everywhere, especially on Ludwig Strasse as it opened into Odeon Platz. I stopped before the Hof Kapelle, with its Byzantine architecture which was known and admired by all in Europe. Inside, I saw three circular arches, three domed roofs, altars, and niches all in their glory. On the walls and ceilings were enormous frescoes. In one, King Saul, a dark and moody man, was featured trying to catch the sun, but he could not do so because of his portrayed immobility. Looking up at the cupola, I could see the fresco of God as the creator, surrounded by the Virgin Mary, Peter, Paul, and Moses. Turning, I saw on the walls portraits of George, Hubert, Louis, Theresa, and other nobles of famous Bavarian families. All this beauty was designed and created by Leo von Kenze and Henrich von Hess, two of the craftsmen I was to contact; it was December 13, 1852.

Making my contacts, I found that neither Kenze nor Hess was willing to accept me as a Wanderjahrer. However, they directed me to Wilhelm von Kulbach, who was another famous Bavarian artist and one of their colleagues. When I arrived at his home, I found that the grounds around his house had fallen into ruins, and his grape vineyards were in desperate need of attention. From a quick glance, it seemed to me that he needed more my knowledge of what I had learned on the farm than what I had studied with Junginger in Freiburg. His wife met me and ushered me into his studio. He talked with me at great length but explained that he had nothing for me to do. However, he was a very gracious man and suggested that, since I would not be saying in Munich, it would be a pity if I left without seeing the city's art. I accepted his offer without telling him that I had already seen some before I arrived at his home.

After we had eaten his wife's elegantly prepared lunch, we set out on a short tour. We walked down Ludwig Strasse to the Triumphal Arch and paused before the Jesuit College, where Kulbach had just finished some mural restorations. As we went to look at his work, we passed many sculptures of poets, philosophers, and legislators. Finally, we came to Kulbach's work. It was outstanding. We then proceeded to the Ruhmeshalle near the Isar River which runs through the city. It was a beautiful Doric Building, designed by Kenze. Construction began in 1850 and was still in progress. The statues were created by the sculptor, Schwanthaler, from marble brought from Utesburg. The building was conceived to honor man's engineering ability, his interaction with the earth. I saw scenes of cattle, alpine activity, vineyards, fishing, navigation, iron working, and the cultivation of corn all interwoven into artistic form. Later, we went to the Basilica of Saint Boniface, which in 1850 had celebrated its Silberne Hochzeit. Kulbach said, "At the time of the basilica's silver anniversary, I told the people of Munich that it took 15 years to decorate this church with the arabesque, frescoes, sculptures, and carvings in wood which they had come that day to see." While there, I mentioned to Kulbach that I was most impressed by the fresco which depicted the Martyrdom of Saint Stephen. This was the kind of art which I hoped some day that I would create.

When we left the basilica, we returned to Kulbach's studio, and he signed my book and again extended his regrets that work would not be available. I reported to the police, and they encouraged me to continue on to my next town.

Next, I went to Landshut but found no work. Quickly I moved to Regensburg, arriving there on December 19. Preparations were being made in the churches for the Christmas celebration; help was needed with the decorations. I remained there until after Christmas, and then I went to Nuremburg. Again, I received the no work available sign; and, discouraged, I was just about ready to quit my Wanderjahre program when I was told that work could be found in Hof, which was the next city on my schedule. I arrived on January 2 and worked until February 4, a good way to start the new year of 1853. After my stay in Hof, I was rejected at Plauen, but, subsequently, did find interesting gilding assignments in Dresden and Leipzig.

On April 24, I registered in Hamburg. There I found my first steady job since I left home. For nine months I would not have to travel. Hamburg was the largest port city of Europe, and some of the richest merchants lived there. Immediately, I could see that the citizens believed in practical realities, and they were very undogmatic with a true sense of open-mindedness and fairness.

Hamburg had come into existence in the year 825 A.D. with the construction of the castle, Hammaburg, which was located between the Alster and Elbe Rivers. The village quickly grew up around the castle; but, in the year 845, the Vikings burned it to the ground. Many people referred to Hamburg as the Phoenix of Europe because, in the 300 years following the Viking invasion, the city burned eight times and each burning was followed by a rebirth in which it was made larger than it had been before. Before I arrived in 1853, the city had experienced its most recent disastrous fire in 1842. I found that the restoration was continuing enthusiastically. Everywhere, there were buildings with ornate rooms whose walls and ceilings needed the services of the fresco painter and gilder. Amongst these were the Bank of Hamburg constructed in 1619, the Grand German Opera House founded in 1678, the Thalia Theater developed in 1843, and the Saint Pauli Theater built in 1841. All these had been damaged in the fire. There were also many splendid Baroque houses, the homes of rich merchants, on the densely populated Brooke Island between the Alster and Elbe Rivers. In these the gilders and decorators were feverishly working.

The first convoy system of shipping to be developed in Europe was established in Hamburg in 1662. By 1853, there were more than 1000 ships in the merchant fleet. Great Men-of-War naval vessels were constructed there. They became part of the Hamburg Navy and sailed each year in convoy with the merchant vessels to ports in South and Central America, East and West Africa, and East Asia. Ship building and repair were unending occupations at the port. All these ships had ornate rooms as living quarters for the officers and respected merchants who sailed the great oceans. It was here that my talents and experience were put to work assisting in an extensive redecoration program.

When I had gained some security and permanency, I was again able to participate in the athletic activities of the Turners. The Turnerschaft in Hamburg was composed of many Turnvereine. Each year, it participated in several athletic events particularly the annual row against the British quartered in the city. It should be understood that Hamburg was not part of any other German state. It was a free, Hanseatic city with a tradition of particularism and self government. It catered to foreign trade and graciously invited foreigners to live and mingle with the native Hamburgers. Naturally, athletics and gymnastics were recreation and diversion for all, foreigners as well as natives.

Each year the Turnerschaft of Hamburg held a huge Turnfest, in which national and international groups entered into athletic competition. Prizes were awarded and festivities, including eating, drinking, singing, and dancing, were enjoyed by all. At these events, I became friendly with many diverse people. We freely and openly discussed the Revolution of 1848 and the possibilities of establishing a Republic for all the German states. I found many who had opinions similar to mine and were convinced that the German states and kingdoms would remain backward unless more freedom were given to the laboring class. Some expressed ideas similar to those of Karl Marx, who in certain intellectual circles was very popular. However, most Germans could not completely accept his kind of socialistic program. We also discussed the progressive movement in the Americas. Many sailors talked of the productivity that they had seen in the ports of the New World. They described the economic successes in several German colonies which had been established in North and South America and the increased emigration of Germans to these colonies. The emigrants were being weaned away from Europe by stories of prosperity and freedom abroad.

In December 1853, my work in Hamburg ended. With the coming of winter, activity at the port slowed exceedingly. Again I was required to travel, but I was advised that, if I returned to Hamburg in February or March, work would be made available to me. In nine days, I passed through six cities: Luebeck, Kelstorf, Kiegel, Rendsburg, Treets, Schleswig, and Flensburg. I reached Flensburg on December 20 and participated in the seasonal Christmas decorating; but, after the holidays, I was moving again. From January 2 until February 4, I found only meager amounts of work as I traveled to and through Copenhagen, Husum, Itzehoe, Glueckstadt, and Elmshorn. On February 4, I was back in Hamburg. I was re-employed at the shipyard. This time, my work period extended to December 12, 1854. Unfortunately, at that time, Hamburg decided to withdraw from the Zollverein and cancel its participation in the Wanderschaft. I was forced to make a serious decision. If I stayed in Hamburg and kept working, I would have to withdraw from my Wanderjahre program. I could then have been hired as an Auslaender. I decided to give up the work and leave. I made this decision five days before I finally left the city. As I stood on the Lombard Bridge looking across the Inner Alster River, I could see the towers of the five great churches (Saint Michael, Saint Jacobi, Saint Peter, Saint Katherine, and Saint Nikolai) silhouetted in the evening sky. That evening, I prayed, "Dear God, you and Hamburg have been good to me, but I must go. I want to finish what I started out to do!"

I left the city on December 14 and completed my Wanderjahre schedule at Hannover, Heidelberg, and Offenburg. I returned to Karlsruhe in January and had my Wanderbuch reviewed by the authorities. I had met 35 masters and had received employment and recommendation from 16 of them. This was sufficient for the ministries to accept my Wanderjahre as a success; my education was complete. Minister Frederick von Holer signed my book on January 11, 1855. Finally, I was an approved craftsman with all the rights and privileges to function in Freiburg and other towns of Breisgau. I had worked 730 complete days in two years and ten months. I returned home with a savings of $80. It was with this stake that I made a down payment on my future.

All through the rest of the winter, I made every effort to establish my practice and propose work programs for the next year. The competition was extreme and the financial situation in Breisgau was at a low ebb. I was not fortunate enough to be associated with an aging master who in retirement would offer me his practice.

With the Turners in Freiburg, I discussed our former members who had emigrated to America, and I read their letters; they described prosperity and unrestricted work opportunities. More and more, I became discouraged; and, one day, I confided in my sister, Francesca. I told her how the American Turners had founded a Turnverein in New York City and, through their organization, were helping the immigrants to have a good quality of life. She could see that I had more reasons for leaving Forchheim than I did to stay. She said, "Erhard, why do you not go to America and take me with you?" We told our parents of our decisions; it was not an easy task, and we received much opposition. Angrily, they replied to me, "Your leaving is surprise enough but to talk Francesca into going with you is an unforgivable sin." Francesca tried to convince them that she truly wanted to emigrate. She said, "This is not only Erhard's idea; it is mine also." However, they did not wish to believe her. We stood firm. Reluctantly, they agreed to let us seek passage for New York in the spring of that year.

I learned that 584,000 Germans had left the fatherland from the port cities of Hamburg, Bremen, and Le Havre for the Americas. Francesca and I were well aware of the Forchheim families that had emigrated from these ports, and several neighbors advised that it would be wise for us to travel through France and depart from Le Havre. Their reasoning was based on knowledge of the economic and social conditions that influenced travel to the port cities.

In the hills north and west of the Alsatian city of Strasbourg, which was 60 miles north of Forchheim, lived many farm people known also as Outworkers. They were hired by a Verlager, an entrepreneur who offered and distributed to them weaving contracts. These they completed during the winter months and the remuneration for their work brought them enough revenue to buy seeds in the spring. Before 1835, most Outworkers spun flax and wove linen, but, by 1855, Alsace had become one of the leading areas in Europe in the manufacture of cotton products. Raw cotton was brought to Le Havre and shipped by wagon train to the hills around Strasbourg. The Verlager distributed the raw material to the Outworkers, and collected and returned the finished products back to Le Havre.

Each spring, large wagon trains in convoy left Strasbourg for Paris loaded with these products. They were then shipped by barge to Le Havre and finally found their way to all ports in the world, especially America. There was always more room on these ships for the return trip to America than there was when the raw materials were imported. The extra room provided excellent passage space for the emigrants. Such travel was very lucrative for the shipping companies. In fact, it was so lucrative that they set up travel agencies, and promoters would visit the towns and villages in Baden, encouraging emigration. For each person the promoter would sign up, he would receive a generous commission. In April, 1855, Francesca and I made arrangements with a shipping company for passage on a ship that was to leave Le Havre in May for New York City. I wrote letters to my Turner friends in New York and gave them the details of our plans.

In the middle of April, Francesca and I went by rail to Offenburg. From there, we traveled to Kehl by wagon, boarded the ferry, crossed the Rhine River, and entered Strasbourg. There, we joined the merchants' convoy for Paris. From Strasbourg, we went to Nancy, traveled to Saint Dizier, and proceeded to Châlons-sur-Marne. The trip was slow, and it was important to stay with the caravan. As long as we were with it, we were under the protection of the merchants and did not have to show any papers to the local authorities. The French gendarmes had come to accept the flood of German emigrants to the port cities as routine. If trouble did arise, the promoter was present to offer the acceptable bribes. From Châlons-sur-Marne, we proceeded on to Chateau-Thierry. Finally, we reached Paris. The merchandise and immigrants, after a wait of ten days, were loaded on barges for their cruise down the Seine River. While waiting for the barge to leave, we camped near the river in the gardens around the Louvre. We reached Le Havre on the 28th day after we left Forchheim.

Upon arrival, we found the likes of a German village; German innkeepers, German merchants, and German ship agents were everywhere. However, the place was not like the quiet, well-disciplined village of Forchheim. Some people were stealing and others were gambling constantly. Many had miscalculated the cost of the ocean travel and turned to crime to find money to pay their ship fare or to pay for a return trip to Baden. Women without husbands were raped, and men without wives were victims of shootings and knifings. Police protection was scanty. The French authorities were little concerned about the masses of people who were not their own. Since safety was found in a respectable hotel, Francesca and I stayed at L'Agneau Blanche, the White Lamb Hotel, at Rue Percanville 51; we waited nine days.

On May 16, 1855, we set sail on a packet ship. Her port of registration was New Orleans; but, on her return trip to America, she was going to make stops at New York, Philadelphia, and Charleston before returning to her home port. Many family groups were well prepared for the voyage with their meat salted, bread baked, cheese prepared, and butter neatly packed in kegs. Personal gear was stored in large chests with great iron bands and heavy locks. The ship's company provided the passengers only with biscuits, rice, and potatoes, but the passengers were allowed to bring their own supplies if they so desired. Many had packed hams, herring, flour, coffee, eggs, vinegar, chocolate, tea, and wine. Fuel was supplied and cooking could be done on board in good weather. We were warned not to make the trip without our own chamber pot (a portable toilet) and a lantern. I was at sea less than a day when I found out how necessary these were!

The passenger deck was two tiers with six-foot berths. Our luggage was scattered everywhere and there was no place to hang our clothes. When we were on the berth deck, we found ourselves amid deck gear, livestock, chickens, and horses hanging in cradles. When we were confined below deck, we found cramped quarters where it was impossible to eat our cheese and biscuits in comfort; and, while sailing the rough North Atlantic, we were below deck very often.

Our voyage was filled with sickness, storms, hatches battened down, bad days, poor ventilation, and foul odors. Sometimes, the berths would appear to be collapsing, kegs were stove in, and bags of peas burst all over the baggage, which was usually soaked and broken. Those who tried to cook on deck, while the ship was pitching and creaking, found that with a sudden surge their stove would be carried overboard. Monotony was like an infectious disease. We had 12 weeks of listening to the everlasting sounds of the creaking of timbers, the shouts and curses of the sailors, and the wash of water against the hull. Only when the sea was calm, and that was not often, could we relax, play cards, shoot marbles, or indulge in a game of dominoes.

Unfortunately, the ship was not without sin. The captain was not God, and sometimes you thought only God could be the last judge and ruler of all. Thieves stole food and property. Some young girls were hired by the officers of the crew for a price that ended their virginity. The rich bribed cooks, and the brutes and bullies attacked the weak. Committees were formed to establish rules of proper conduct, but enforcement was limited. The committees offered weak reprimands for young couples accused of illegal romance; but one time they prevailed upon the captain to incarcerate in the brig a bully who victimized a fellow passenger.

Excitement on board usually resulted from simple things. A sudden cry, "cat overboard" or "child down the hatchway," brought blanket covered passengers to their feet. Shouts like "whales in the water" or "icebergs off the starboard bow" started a chain of excitement that ended after a day's conversation.

Death occurred on our voyage; and, when it did, the captain ordered the body wrapped in sail cloth, weighted with sand, placed on the plank at high bulwark, and dropped into the ocean. The ship never paused in a good wind and the minister read "windfully" from the Bible; eight people died on our crossing, including two new born babies.

Sundays broke the monotony. We put on good clothing, steerage was fumigated with vinegar, coal pots were burned to ventilate, and a prayer meeting was held at which flute and violin were played. Sunday was a day for God and the people he had created. Sunday was the day we all hoped our resurrection would come since most other days were our Good Fridays.

On July 4, we learned how Americans loved their land. The ship's crew celebrated their Independence Day; sailors ran flags up the yard arm and salutes were fired. The captain ordered a pig killed and roasted; each of us received a share. In the evening, fireworks burst into the sky, and many danced to flute and violin well into the night.

As the days extended into weeks and added up to months, homesickness and discouragement enveloped the group. Many voiced the same thought, "Our old home is so far away, and our new home never seems to come!" Finally, the new home arrived. A first glimpse of America was the lighthouse off Montauk Point! The passengers were like children at the first Christmas they could understand. Bells were rung as the pilot boat was seen approaching our vessel. We knew that we were approaching New York, and our long ordeal was coming to an end.

After passing through the strait between Brooklyn and Staten Island, we anchored in the harbor. We went ashore. Our first stop in America was Castle Garden, an old opera house that was converted into an immigration center. It was located on a little island at the tip of Manhattan Island, and across the channel we could see the green grass in Battery Park. Later, I discovered that Jenny Lind, the famous Swedish singer, had made her American debut there in 1850.

When we came ashore, Francesca and I met the families of our Turner friends whom we had written to before leaving Europe. For several days, they had been watching the shipping schedules in the *New York Times*. They helped us while we were processed. Alas! What a chore it was! We were uncomfortable and embarrassed with the medical examinations. The paperwork seemed endless. However, there was a great difference between interrogation in America as compared to that in Europe. America was loud; Europe was quiet. In Europe, we sat still, and the investigator did the questioning. At Castle Garden, our Turner friends, who impregnated English with a Baden dialect, seemed to overpower the investigator. They talked loudly, and he met the challenge, shouted back, banged on the table, but always gave the impression he was taking care of us. Francesca turned to me and said, "This is confusion. Is all America going to be confusion?" In two days, it was all over, we were disposed of, and we were free to go anywhere we wished. It was a good feeling!

For four years, Francesca and I lived together in New York City. Our first residence was at the Konstanz, a hotel on William Street in lower Manhattan Island. It was owned and operated by Max Weber. He was a graduate of the Karlsruhe Military Academy. During the Revolution of 1848, he defected from Duke Leopold's army, fought with the revolutionists under Sigel, and fled to America. Later, we moved to an apartment on Platt Street. We had two bedrooms and an indoor toilet. The kitchen had a wash sink which we used for bathing, dish washing, and laundering. A small sitting room was also included. We paid $68 a year for the apartment.

New York was a city of about 0.8 million people, mostly living in the lower tip of Manhattan Island. Brooklyn was a separate city, as was Williamsburg. North of Manhattan were the small communities of Yorkville, Manhattanville, and Harlem. The city of New York ended at the southern edge of Central Park, which was under construction. Broadway was the main street; and, in the morning and evening, the traffic was curb to curb. When we first arrived, we were transported through the streets on 30 seat omnibuses, but these were soon replaced by modern horse cars. At times traffic was so congested that it took 20 minutes to cross the street. Bleeker Street was the dividing line between the Haves and Have Nots. Many rich and notable people lived to the north of it; and, to the south, we found sleazy gambling houses on Park Row, Barclay Street, and Versey Street. At one time, 6,000 such establishments were devoted to the art of fleecing the pleasure seeker. Faro and raffles were the prime amusements.

East of Broadway beyond Anthony Street lay the slums, the homes of many rowdy Irishmen. These spread over to the East River, curled around the southern tip of Manhattan Island, and proceeded upward to East 42nd Street. In this area, I found a sprawling mass of filthy tenements. The center was at Five Points, the intersection of five streets: Anthony, Little Water, Orange, Cross, and Mulberry. The intersection was called Paradise Square; later, it was named Columbus Square. Nearby was an endless number of pawnbrokers, children who were ragged and barefoot, beggars, thieves, drunkards, and sex offenders. They lived in tenements with dark and dank cellars where tunnels led to the sewers; rats and disease were rampant.

Another ghetto was located near Gotham Square, the intersection of Cherry, Water, and Roosevelt Streets. Day and night, police patrolled this area in squads of six or more. The most notorious drinking stop was Sweeney's Shambles, an Irish tavern at 36 Cherry Street. Out of these two despicable areas grew the powerful political machine called Tammany Hall. William Marcy Tweed, who began his career as a fireman on the Bowery, was the leader.

My first artistic painting was done for Lorenzo Delmonico. His restaurant was located at the corner of Fifth Avenue and 14th Street. I earned $1 a day. The first $1 bill I earned I saved to send home to my parents in Forchheim. I also found employment at Horace Greely's home at 35 East 19th Street and at Edwin Forrest's home at 436 West 22nd Street. Edwin was a well known actor married to Catherine Sinclair.

Later, when I teamed up with Enrico Tassi, an Italian immigrant from Milano, my services and his were accepted by the ruling class of the city: the Rhinelanders, the Schermerhornes, the Gracies, and the Joneses. Besides enjoying fine art on their walls, these families also imported French chefs and the latest apparel from Paris. As employees, we also did frescoes and decorations in the Rococo Mansions on Fifth Avenue.

These mansions were noted for their large and ornate ballrooms, banquet halls, and art galleries. Leonard Jerome, a Wall Street tycoon, was so extravagant that he placed carpeting on the floor of his stables, paneling made of black walnut on his walls, and a vast number of plate glass mirrors throughout his house.

Tassi and I invented a novel art form for churches. We implanted a Heilige Geist, a dove surrounded by golden rays, in the ceiling of Saint Anthony Church south of Bleeker Street. First, we painted the scene on canvas. Then, we set up our scaffold, carried the finished canvas up to the ceiling and glued it in place. Then, we applied to it the stirred-chromatic method of Obergarth von Fuchs. After we retouched and glazed it, one would think that we had painted the entire scene directly onto the ceiling as Michaelangelo did with his paintings in the Sistine Chapel.

While I worked with Enrico, Francesca was a maid at Eugen Lievre's Shakespeare Hotel at Duane and William Streets. In 1858 a merchant from Philadelphia, George Zell, came to New York and stayed at the hotel. He became attracted to Francesca, they corresponded, and they were married in 1859. Subsequently, they made their home in Philadelphia. On one occasion, Tassi and I spent an extended period of time there, doing artistic decorations in one of George's stores. In 1860, Francesca and George decided to make a trip to Europe. She was anxious to show off her new husband to our parents in Forchheim; Francesca and George departed in the spring.

During our first four years in New York City, Francesca and I found the German ethnic group very active. Socializing with them allowed us to express ourselves in a friendly culture. The Turnverein was its center; but, in America, we simply called it the Verein. The official language of the Verein was German. The use of the language was approved by the membership, and its use was a great help to us because it served to bridge the gap between us newcomers and those who had been previously Americanized. However, by speaking German and primarily socializing with our own kind, we encouraged prejudice and experienced much intolerance.

I joined the Verein, immediately after I arrived in New York City. Its Turnhalle, first called National Hall, was located at 29-31 Canal Street, near Broadway. In May, 1856, it moved to a larger hall on the corner of Christie and Delancy Streets and moved back again in 1858. This moving back and forth was dependent upon the whims of landlords. The Verein did not have sufficient funds to purchase its own property. However, through $1 a year additional taxation of the membership and the floating of a stock issue in denominations of $10 per share, its building fund reached a sum of $14,000 by 1859. On February 16, 1859, the Quaker Church at 27-33 Orchard Street was purchased for $30,000. On completing some renovations, the Verein was able to establish its headquarters there on July 13. Two more structures were added to each side of the original building, and, early in 1861, the complex became the Verein's permanent Turnhalle. Ten years later, this property was sold, and the Verein moved to more elegant quarters as the German population became more prosperous and began to relocate uptown.

During those antebellum years, we practiced the exercises at the Turnhalle but did not participate in National Turnfeste. In 1856, a split took place in the Turnerbund, the National Turner Organization, as it divided into two contending philosophical and political factions. The New York Turnverein did not agree with the views of either faction and withdrew. After the Civil War, with reorganization and differences of opinions compromised, the New Yorkers rejoined the Turnerbund and participated in the first postbellum Turnfest held in Baltimore in June, 1867.

The philosophy and ideals of our Verein were deeply influenced by the 36 Acht-und-vierziger, who founded the organization on June 6, 1850. Recall, Constantin Rosswog, from Endingen, was one of these. Shortly after arriving in America, the group met at Stubenbord's Restaurant in Duane Street and established the Socialistischer Turnverein. This later became The New York Turnverein. The members elected Sigismund Kaufmann as their First Speaker. From this time on, he threw all his talents and energy into the Turner Movement in America and was elected the first president of the Turnerbund. In 1870, as a leader in the Republican Party, he was its candidate for the office of Lieutenant Governor for the State of New York.

The founders chose to call Kaufmann a First Speaker rather than a president or chairman. This was to symbolize their devotion to democracy and opposition to tyranny and dictatorship. As First Speaker, Kaufmann was to speak for the members; this meant he was to represent them but not rule them. His authority was considered to be derived from the members and was to be exercised only by their consent. The Acht-und-vierziger's fear of dictatorship was so great that, for the first 20 years, the First Speaker's term of office was only six months. However, he could be, and was repeatedly, re-elected. Kaufmann held this post on five different occasions between 1850 and 1867.

The founders' ideals are further illustrated in a prelude to the constitution which they wrote for the Verein. They said, "We stand on a revolutionary and socialistic foundation." By revolutionary, they meant striving for the freedom which prompted the American Revolution of 1776 and resulted in the establishment of a Union. These Acht-und-vierziger had just come from Europe and were political refugees of the ill-fated German Revolution of 1848, which in its demise failed to unite the 39 autonomous states. What they lost abroad, they found in America and were all very willing to promote and defend.

Their socialistic ideas, which were populistic rather than Marxian, were revealed in their active promotion of the rights of the working man. They claimed that all laborers had the right to organize into unions and to regulate their hours of weekly labor. They further promoted the emancipation of women; the unfettered right of free speech, press, and assemblage; direct election of United States senators; taxation on the basis of ability to pay; abolition of slavery; and ultimate abolition of the Senate and presidency, substituting for the latter an executive committee of the House of Representatives. With the exception of the last of these, all have become common practice in the United States.

Although gymnastics were of primary importance at our Turnhalle, informal and social gatherings were also held, especially on Saturday nights. And even amid our deutsche Gemuetlichkeit, we had informal discussions on serious subjects such as the political situation in America and in the fatherland. Eventually, we made these discussions formal and called them Geistliches Turnen or mental gymnastics. We also formed two special groups, the singing section (Liedertafel) and the dramatic section. Practice in these groups followed the Turning Exercises on Wednesday nights. Heinicke, Krueger, and Heimer were the first conductors of the Liedertafel. They often said, "Gehoert doch das deutsche Lied unzertrennlich zum Turnen." With these words, they expressed their desire to hear a German song that really was a Turner song.

As with the gymnastics, competition and reward in the cultural area were considered basic, and became features of our Turnfeste. Heinrich Metzner, who also was continuously re-elected as First Speaker, won the laurel wreath in the field of literary work at the Bundesturnfest held in Baltimore in 1867.

Further, we realized the necessity of educating our young members. So, we established a library and a school at the Turnhalle. In 1857, we had four faculty members, and Doctor Gartner was the principal. Our school was tuition free for children of the Verein members. All elementary subjects were taught in German and English, and students could elect courses in bookkeeping, singing, and French.

Our female members participated in a special way. Francesca joined the group of Verein ladies known as the Turnschwestern. She remained active with them until she moved to Philadelphia with George Zell. This ladies auxiliary of the Verein held regular meetings and organized many social activities that raised money to finance the needs of the gymnasts, the dramatic group, and the singing group. It also was influential in aiding the Verein in procuring the down payment on the Orchard Street property.

Although much of our social life did center around the Turnhalle, Francesca and I also participated in many of the glamorous and world embracing events that took place in New York City. On August 5, 1858, President Buchanan sent the first telegraph message to Queen Victoria over the Transatlantic Wire Cable. At first, the experiment seemed to be a failure; but, when a reply finally arrived from the Queen, the whole city broke into celebration. Bells rang from the tower of Trinity Church, cannons were fired, and fireworks were displayed. The Crystal Palace was crowded with elegantly dressed people and the city was illuminated. Many speeches were delivered, torch light processions were conducted, and 50,000 enthusiasts crossed the North and East Rivers to join in the celebrations. The joy was short lived. On September 25, the cable broke for the third time, and the *New York Times* condemned the Federal Government for wasting $1.8 million. Later, that autumn, the Crystal Palace caught fire; and, even though 2,000 people escaped, the building sustained $2 million in damages.

The newspapers kept us aware of the slavery problem in America. The slave trade was illegal, but it was still practiced. It was dramatically exposed in 1858 when the *Haidee* sank off the coast of Long Island near Montauk Point. Nine hundred blacks were aboard the ship, and most of these were lost. After the ship went down, many sailors who made shore safely were discovered wandering around Long Island freely disposing of Spanish Doubloons. They were attempting to exchange them for Yankee whiskey.

On October 18, 1859, a well-meaning man, John Brown, made an attack on the United States Arsenal at Harper's Ferry, a small village on the border of Maryland and Virginia. He wanted to procure weapons and ammunition so that he could give them to black slaves. He planned for the slaves to revolt against their masters. He was unsuccessful, and eventually he was hanged. For a brief time, New Yorkers were disturbed over the news of this raid, but they soon forgot it. Their attention turned to local politics. Fernando Wood, who held troops at bay on the steps of City Hall in 1857, was again elected mayor of New York City. He had carried on a raucous but crowd-pleasing campaign.

The arrival of prominent ships and people was usually a time of great excitement in New York City. In 1860, the largest steam vessel ever built, humorously called *Brunel's Folly*, made her maiden voyage from Milwall, England, to New York. The ship was actually known as the *Great Eastern*. It arrived in July. When it docked in the North River, swarms of people flocked to see it. On that day, I saw more food and drink sold at one time than ever before in my life. Dadworth's Band played, and there was dancing in the streets late into the night.

Also, in the summer of 1860, Albert Edward, the Prince of Wales, son of Queen Victoria and Prince Albert, visited New York. This was the first British celebrity of any stature to visit America since the colonists revolted against the crown. New Yorkers were ready for a big party. They paraded the prince to City Hall, Trinity Church, and the Cooper Union. Speeches were made, and the day ended with the traditional fireworks. Similar celebrations were held when Garibaldi arrived in search of Italian-American recruits to fight for Italian unification and when the Japanese Embassy was first established.

On September 10, 1860, Francesca and George arrived in Forchheim; the villagers celebrated! Francesca informed my parents of my success and gave my mother and father the first $1 bill I had earned. It was a green, oversized note redeemable for its equivalent in silver. That note was never cashed and still exists in Forchheim. I was 29 years old, not rich like a Rhinelander, a Schermerhorne, a Gracie, or a Jones, but I was proud and happy. Work was plentiful, and I enjoyed my companionship with Enrico Tassi.

Suddenly, my romance with the New World was shattered by stark reality. South Carolina seceded from the Union and fired her cannons on Fort Sumter. President Lincoln called upon the northern states to recruit 75,000 militiamen. Although the militia was intended to be short term and used for the defense of the capital, the New York Turnverein held a war meeting and organized a volunteer regiment, which would fight alongside the United States Army. I volunteered immediately. I was a long way from the fatherland, happy in my adopted country, and now by choice der Turner Soldat. In becoming the Turner Soldier, I did not make that choice out of a spirit of adventure but out of a spirit consistent with my origin, experience, ideals, and love for the Union and Constitution that promoted and protected the individual rights of all men.

My fellow Turners, who had similar origins, experiences, and ideals, did the same. We may have spoken a different language than our nativistic brothers, and we may have had habits and a culture which they did not understand; but, as my history herein recorded shows, we could demonstrate our good education, generosity in our impulses, wholesomeness in our reactions, and stalwartness in our adversity. We were then asked, as were our nativistic brothers, to bring our strong sense of duty and devotion for country and cause to the battlefields of the American Civil War.

Unfortunately, our regimental history does not exist. Neither the veterans of our regiment nor subsequent members of the participating Turnvereine ever composed a detailed account of our activities in the war. I believe my construction of the regimental history will help to fill the void. However, I will accept hesitantly and fearfully the assignment. The story contains some embarrassing facts which for many reasons, mainly emotional, could neither have been written before the 19th century faded nor in the 20th century before the demise of our last noble veteran.

Top: A map of 19th Century Europe. Baden is the small German state on the border of France, north of Switzerland. Bottom: The Kaiserstuhl and its surroundings. The Black Forest is in the background. Forchheim is the village surrounded by small farms near Endingen.

Top: Marie M. Miller (1974) viewing the grave of Martin Futterer, mayor of Forchheim, Germany, 1811-1826. Bottom: Marie M. Miller standing before the birthplace of Erhard Futterer, her grandfather, in Forchheim, Germany.

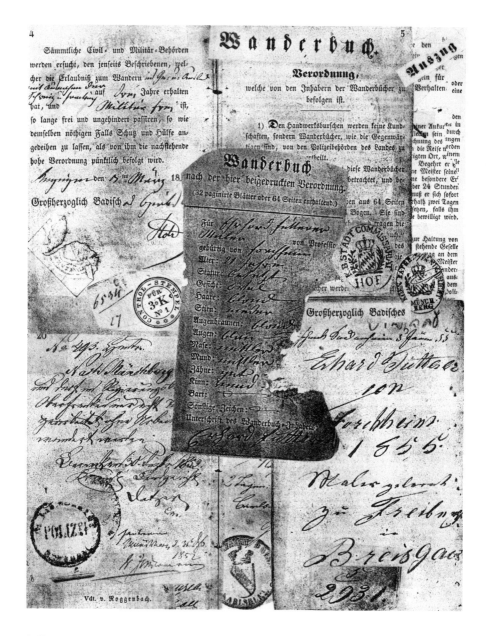

Collage of selected pages from Erhard Futterer's Wanderbuch. A German apprentice in each of the crafts carried one of these on his Wanderjahre. A completed book was like a present day diploma. A successful Wanderjahre rendered the apprentice his mastercraftman's license.

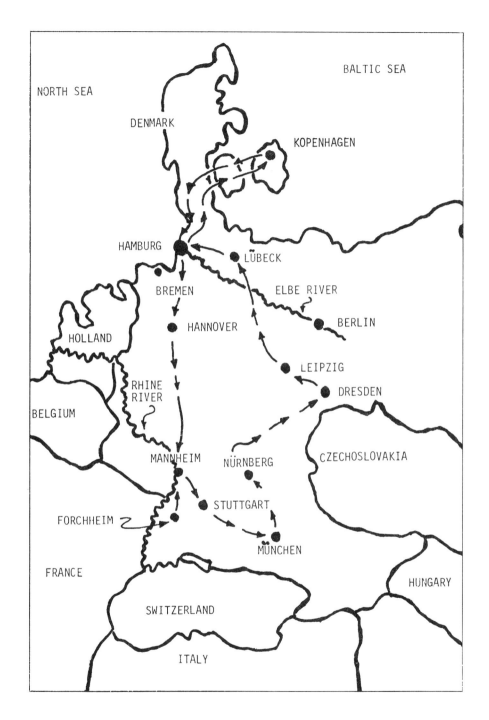

Travel route in central Europe assigned to Erhard Futterer for his Wanderjahre (1852-1855).

New York City, 1861
Left: Crowded Broadway   Right: South Street Docks

SIGISMUND KAUFMANN

HEINRICH METZNER

HERMAN BENNECKE

Turnhalle, New York
Turnverein, 1861
and
Distinguished Turners
Mentioned in the Treatise

GUSTAV SCHOLER

Top: City Hall in New York City. The United Turner Rifles had its departure ceremony here on June 13, 1861. It was the largest celebration given to a German regiment leaving New York City. Bottom: Fifth Avenue and Twenty-eight Street, New York City. Erhard Futterer and Enrico Tassi painted frescoes in these mansions.

THE FIRST YEAR OF WAR

On April 16, 1861, I wrote to my parents in Forchheim and informed them that Francesca and George should not delay in returning to America. I tried to explain where Fort Sumter, South Carolina, was located and how war had erupted in America between the North and the South. I related that Mr. Lincoln, our President, had called upon the northern states to provide 75,000 men to defend the capital; he was going to stand firm against secession and not allow the Union to crumble. Francesca and George sailed from Le Havre on July 3, 1861. They arrived in Philadelphia while I was der Turner Soldat in camp at Fortress Monroe.

Long before Abraham Lincoln was inaugurated, in March, 1861, war clouds hung over the country. During the election in November, 1860, several prominent southern political leaders warned that the South would secede if he were elected. In December, 1860, many southern members of President James Buchanan's Cabinet resigned. Control over Federal arsenals in the southern states fell into the hands of southern sympathizers and unrest was brewing amongst the cadets and officers at West Point Military Academy.

Our Turners' first serious encounter with southern rage took place in Baltimore, a city close to the capital. In the spring of 1861, it was a seedbed of hatred for the Yankees, a word used to designate those who favored the Federal Government. On April 19, the Stars and Stripes had been removed from all public buildings in the city and replaced by the Maryland state flag. The Baltimore Turnverein refused to take down its national flag. A mob gathered in the streets around the Turnhalle, and demanded the Stars and Stripes be removed. From the balcony, the Verein's president shouted to the rioters, "We will defend our flag! We would rather blow up this building than disgrace it by raising a Rebel standard!" The mob dispersed but returned the next day and stormed the building. They ransacked the rooms, broke windows, and threw the gymnastic equipment into the street. The *Turnzeitung*, the national Turner newspaper, had its headquarters there. The mob clubbed the office staff, destroyed the presses, and razed the building to the ground. Many prominent Verein members fled the city in fear of being taken hostage and murdered.

News of the tragedy spread rapidly and the northern Turnvereine were outraged. War meetings and councils were immediately called or planned. The impact of these councils would subsequently be felt since the Turner membership would positively respond to Lincoln's call to arms. Knowledge of why such a positive response would be expected lies in an understanding of the development of the Turner organization in America and its rapid growth and influence on the German immigrant population.

The first Turnverein in America was founded by Friedrich Hecker at Cincinnati in 1848. He was 37 years old, a well educated man, a great orator, and a political refugee from Baden. At the outbreak of the German Revolution of 1848, he spoke out publicly and forcefully to establish freedom for the farmers and the middle class and denounced the persecution of the Jews. After a highly emotional oratorical defense of freedom given at Kandern, Baden, he was pursued by Duke Leopold's Army and forced to flee the country. He came to America and stayed with friends in the German colony at Belleville, Illinois. He solicited contributions for the revolutionists in the fatherland and returned to Baden in 1849.

Upon arrival in Europe, he found that the Frankfurt Parliament was to be dissolved, and he returned to Belleville, where he became a self-made farmer. At the outbreak of the Civil War, he joined the 3rd Missouri Regiment as a private; but later, at the request of the Illinois Germans, he organized that state's 24th and 82nd Volunteer Regiments. He was wounded at Chancellorsville in 1863, gave honorable service at Missionary Ridge during the Chattanooga campaign, and resigned from the military in 1864. After the war, he continued to serve the German immigrants in the midwest. He had a profound influence on the political thought formulated amongst the Turners, before and after the war.

After the Turnverein was established in Cincinnati, other Turnvereine were quickly organized throughout the American states, both north and south. They came into existence so rapidly that it was necessary to establish a national organization, which was called the Turnerbund, in order to ensure the individual Turnverein's existence and protect its common interest, while preserving its individuality. The communication arm of the Turnerbund was the *Turnzeitung*. It kept the Turnvereine membership informed about conventions, Turnfeste, awards, and the political views of the Turnerbund. When the Turnerbund's national convention was held in Philadelphia in 1854, sixty-two Turnvereine were represented. The following year, at its convention in Buffalo, New York, a political platform promoting three major principles was established. These were accepted by the majority of the membership as Turner doctrine and published in the *Turnzeitung*.

According to this doctrine, the Turners were not to vote at the ballot box for any member of the Know-Nothing Party or for anyone who identified with it. If candidates for national offices wished to receive the endorsement of the Turners, they had to publicly declare themselves in opposition to the nativistic philosophy which was prevalent throughout the country, a philosophy that labeled the immigrants as secondary citizens. The doctrine further declared its opposition to slavery, which was regarded as an institution unworthy of a republic and not in accord with the principles of freedom. Finally, it declared its opposition to prohibition laws of any kind. They were considered undemocratic in theory and not feasible in practice. However, these principles of the Turner doctrine were in tune with the spirit of republicanism which was gaining momentum in America. Disruptively, the convention's opposition to slavery opened the door for dissension amongst its participants. It set northern Turners against their southern brothers five years before Fort Sumter was fired upon.

The spirit of republicanism was one of progress and expansion. The products of invention, investment, and adventure carried the entrepreneur into the territories, sweeping along with him the immigrants, who were the laborers needed to bring his dreams to reality. The immigrant wanted the right of free labor and was resolved not to be bound in employer servitude. He needed power to gain that right and found it in the protection afforded by laws enacted by a strong Federal Government. Hence, at all costs, he wanted the Union to be preserved! He did not want the government to vacillate and compromise with slavery. He proposed that, only if every vestige of that institution was destroyed, could freedom of labor be guaranteed!

Thus, in theory, all young German immigrants were "abolitionists!" They questioned, "If the Supreme Court can make the Negro legal property, could not the immigrant become the legal property of his employer?" On my Wanderjahre, I had to accept the wage offered to me, and my job opportunities were limited by the whim and fancy of a mastercraftsman. I was not allowed to question! Was I not his slave? Working in America, I had freedom of movement and free competition for my services, and I was not limited to the strict confines of my work definition. If, in the South, the notion of slaves' being owned, bought, and sold, using the laws of commerce, persisted without government control, could not the grasping monopolist of the North maintain a dominion over me? It would be more galling than slavery. I would be rented! I would be a victim of wage slavery! I was not naive enough to think that avarice would cease; but, if the concept of slavery were not considered legal by the Federal Government, the avarice could be controlled by law.

The Republican Party was a proponent of free labor and was becoming strong enough to instill a belief in it in American culture. Many of the older Germans, who had immigrated prior to 1840, were drawn to the Republicans. They appreciated their motto, "Where there are no slaves, laboring men are respectable and respected. Where slavery exists, the laborer is not respected."

Most Acht-und-vierziger militantly supported the Republican Party. In 1856, they supported that party's candidate, John Charles Fremont, for President. Their slogan was, "Free Speech, Free Press, Free Soil, Free Work, and Free Kansas!" In that election year, German newspapers in New York, Chicago, Boston, Milwaukee, and St. Louis endorsed Fremont. Some German intellectuals such as Hecker, Haussaurek, Koerner, Froebel, and Schurz openly campaigned for Fremont. They were convinced that he would serve their best interests and that he had the voice of "prophecy and prosperity."

Fremont was the son of a French immigrant who had run off with an American woman. He was born in Georgia in 1813 and, in his early manhood, became a surveyor in the United States Army's Topographical Corps. His surveys revealed the geographic features of the Rocky Mountains, the Oregon Trail, and California. He wrote vivid descriptions of his explorations and speculated possibilities for routes, settlements, railroads, forts, farms, and mines in the far West. He appealed to those active in the expansionist movement and encouraged Americans to think that all the West belonged to them. He proposed that California did not belong to Mexico. He claimed, "War with Mexico is justified!" He joined in the conflict. Later, he settled in California. There, he became a senator when California was admitted as a free state into the Union. Subsequently, he was asked to be the Republican Party's candidate for the presidency. The Democrats used slur tactics in the campaign against him, stressed his illegitimacy, and falsely accused him of being a Catholic. He lost the election to Mr. James Buchanan.

Fremont's campaign failure did not weaken the German interest in republicanism. On the contrary, it paved the way for the support of Lincoln and the Republican platform in 1860. Karl Schurz, chairman of the Wisconsin delegation and member of the Resolutions Committee, was very visible at the Republican convention in Chicago. As a member of that committee, he effected a resolution in the platform which assured that no changes would be made in the rights accorded to the immigrants. After the convention, he openly campaigned for Lincoln, traveling 21,000 miles, east and west, across the country. Francis Lieber, Frederick Muench, and Judge Krekel from Missouri also campaigned vigorously with him.

Not all German immigrants switched to the Republican Party, for some were staunch Democrats, but a great number were swayed by diligent militants led by the Turners. They deeply instilled four ideas into the German community. These were: the Union must be preserved, slavery must be abolished, people must live according to the laws of reason, and republicanism must be entrenched in the continent. When Fort Sumter was attacked, the Turners were convinced that, if the South prevailed, these ideas were in jeopardy and they would have to fight to maintain them.

In order to fight your enemy, you should know him and know why he is so angry that he is willing to kill! If the South was proposing secession, there must be more to her anger than merely disliking tariffs placed against cotton. The North was buying nearly $200 million worth of cotton from the South each year and was selling her pork, corn, flour, beef, and machinery. True, there were tariff laws. Was war to result because of these laws? They could be changed and trade could be better negotiated. Would war be fought because New York was becoming a rival to Charleston? Charleston could become more competitive if she so desired.

I was well aware of my reasons for fighting to preserve the Union. There were 1,545,508 German immigrants in America and the country was attracting more. If the Union crumbled, immigration would cease, and the asylum to the world's oppressed would disappear. This was my fear and it was great! What fear did the brethren in the South have that was just as great? Was it so great that it forced the Southerner to be diametrically opposed to liberalism and progressivism?

However, I could see that the southern philosophy was developed and controlled, in a paternalistic way by the aristocratic plantation owner, and fed to the middle class white man. The southern planter was a supreme despot in his small domain. He owned his land and his labor and had no sense of dependency upon others. His sufficiency was in his land, which produced the money crop for him. He had no industry or enterprise off the plantation, and his sense of obligation was measured only by the benefits he received from the land. He did not develop distant lands and was too land-rich to find the cash for investments. He distrusted the Federal Government, strongly held to his identity, feared the spirit of republicanism, and despised any social organizations different from his own.

In willful ignorance, he developed a stubborn dogmatism, antagonism, and jealousy. This was his identity; it was very real to him and he called it democracy! He believed in the rule of the majority, but he did not have the majority. In Congress, he was represented as only one fiftieth of the whole nation, but his philosophy was that of one half of the whole nation's identity. For 84 years, he colonized, revolutionized, and constructed his empire in cooperation with his northern brethren but never integrated with them. For 84 years, the North seemed satisfied with him and profited from the gifts which came from his land. Now, he was accused of conservatism and warned that his empire would crumble.

Yes, he did not like what he saw, heard, or felt. He was very angry, reacted violently, advocated the primacy of State's Rights, refused to tolerate any more compromises, and sought a solution in secession! To him, it was his constitutional right, and he felt that, as a nation detached from the Union, his State could negotiate with the North in the same manner as any other world nation was doing.

Further, after making his choice to secede, he could not understand why he was not allowed to go his own way, quietly and peacefully. Eventually, he threw away his wisdom and understanding. He allowed his agitation and hatred to replace them and became reckless in his frustration. He said, "If I fight to gain my freedom, I may lose it, but, if I don't fight, I will lose it!" He knew the country could not remain half slave and half free, but he wanted the North to let him have his slaves and be free from being absorbed.

The firing on Fort Sumter ended all debate. The die was cast! The South's great gamble was on! It was based on the expectation that the North would not fight. However, if it did, immigrants were not expected to actively participate, and the North's military strength in numbers would only equal the South's. Moreover, the South was sure she had officer quality which surpassed the North's.

The assumption was wrong! Throughout the North the immigrants responded — Germans, Irish, Swedes, Norwegians, Hungarians, and Slavs. Before the war ended, about 200,000 Germans had fought for the Union cause. New York State sent 36,000 Germans, 11 percent of the total number of citizens who volunteered or were drafted. Twenty percent of the volunteers from Wisconsin were German, as were 10 to 15 percent of the volunteers from Minnesota, Maryland, and New Jersey. Missouri had the largest rate, 36 percent; out of 85,400 volunteers, 30,899 were Germans. It was reported that Robert E. Lee said, "Take the Dutchmen out of the Union army and we can whip those Yankees easily." They were the largest group of foreigners to answer Lincoln's call to arms. Prior to the first battle at Bull Run, five German regiments from New York State, four from Pennsylvania, one from Ohio, and one from Indiana had been formed and placed in uniform. As the war proceeded, fully or almost fully, German regiments came from New York, Pennsylvania, Ohio, Missouri, Illinois, Wisconsin, Indiana, Minnesota, "Loyal Texas," Iowa, and Kentucky.

Our Turners, in great numbers, answered the call to arms. A battalion of Turners from Philadelphia joined the 29th New York Regiment. The 9th Ohio Regiment was a Turner regiment from Cincinnati. Missouri had the Turner Regiment of the West, the 17th, recruited out of St. Louis. Its companies were filled with Vereine members from Cincinnati, Detroit, Milwaukee, Oskosh, Peoria, Keokuk, Davenport, and Gutenberg. Seven states were represented: Missouri, Iowa, Illinois, Ohio, Michigan, Wisconsin, and Pennsylvania. Also, the Turners formed smaller units within state regiments. The Turner Union Cadets of Chicago gave 105 men to Company B in the 24th Illinois Regiment formed by Hecker. The Milwaukee Turnverein sent a battalion of 40 sharpshooters to join the 5th Wisconsin Regiment, which already contained, in Company C, 105 Turners from that state. The 32nd Indiana Regiment had Turners from Indianapolis, Madison, Aurora, Lawrenceburg, Terre Haute, Lafayette, Laporte, and Evansville.

In the latter part of April, Rudolph Kluckhuhn, First Speaker of the New York Turnverein, called a special war council at the Turnhalle. The Turners in Brooklyn, Williamsburg, and Newark had been notified and their officers attended. The hall was jammed to capacity and Kluckhuhn proclaimed, "It is our duty to answer Mr. Lincoln's call to arms. With our cry, Bahn Frei, we can strike a blow to aid the victory of justice, freedom, and the Constitution." A lively discussion followed, and a war committee was formed. It consisted of Kluckhuhn, Bernet, Lorch, Bennecke and Hoyn. A show of hands revealed that New York could fill four companies of a complete regiment. Newark promised two companies. Williamsburg and Brooklyn said that they could combine to form one company.

During the next two weeks, the war committee notified Turnvereine in Albany, Rochester, Syracuse, Union Hill, Hudson, Morrisania, Poughkeepsie, Boston, Bloomingdale, and Saugerties. Their response was immediate and positive. By the end of April, 1861, sufficient members were available to make up ten companies forming a complete regiment of 1,200 men. Some members in Philadelphia, who did not have sufficient numbers for a Pennsylvania regiment, volunteered.

By May 6, 1861, the New York State Committee had approved our regiment along with accepting the 7th and 8th New York Regiments and Ellsworth's Zouaves from the New York City Fire Department. Our muster ceremony took place on Staten Island on May 9. At the ceremony, General William F. Smith received us as a bona fide volunteer regiment in the United States Army for two years. We assumed that our commitment would last until June 3, 1863. Later, we discovered that an error had been made in processing our commitment papers. Five companies, A through E, were legally committed for three months rather than two years. Max Weber was chosen as commander with the rank of colonel; and, by his choice, Francis Weiss was made lieutenant colonel. We were not given a surgeon or a chaplain until July 1, 1861, at which time Julius Hauser became our surgeon, and Gustav Fritz was elected chaplain.

At the time of our enrollment, the 20th New York Regiment, known as the United Turner Rifles, was composed of the following Turnvereine in each Company: Company A, Newark; Company B, New York City; Company C, New York City; Company D, New York City, Albany, Poughkeepsie, and New Jersey; Company E, New York City; Company F, New York City; Company G, New York City, Poughkeepsie, Rochester, Syracuse, Newark, and Boston; Company H, New York City, Brooklyn, Hudson, Morrisania, Saugerties, and Union Hill; Company I, Brooklyn, Williamsburg, College Point, and Philadelphia; Company K, New York City, Brooklyn, Bloomingdale, and New Jersey.

I was assigned as a private in Company B. In our company, Anthony Bracklin was elected captain. Franz Munich was chosen as first lieutenant. Fritz Letzeiser became our ensign and Charles Bleidorn was made first sergeant. The second sergeants were Charles Ludwig and Ernst Pries. Our five corporals were: Henry Bauscher, William Lange, Carl Meyer, William Hofensack, and Henry Blank. John Monk and William Pfretscher were made the company musicians. Monk, who was 19, was the youngest in our company.

At roll call on the day of muster, we had 64 privates who in two years would experience boredom, praise, and condemnation. We would have our fill of officers, events, marches, maneuvers, the enemy, the land and sea we would fight on, and the mosquitoes and graybacks that would feed off our flesh and blood. When it was over, with our ranks depleted with dead, wounded, and missing, we would often recall with sadness that day on the drill field when we naively but enthusiastically responded:

OTTO ADAM, OTTO AHREND, FRANZ ASSMUSS, GEORGE AAB, CHARLES AMEIS, ALBERT BRUST, JOHN BRANDENBURGER, AUGUST BECKER, FRIEDRICK BREITHUT, AUGUST BRUHLMEIER, BERTHOLD BAUER, AUGUST DIETRICH, HENRY EMERICH, LUDWIG FINKELMEYER, OSCAR FETSCH,

BAPTIST FIRMBACH, ERHARD FUTTERER, ALBERT FUCHS, BERNARD GOCKNER, THEODORE GELBART, CHARLES HAEDLER, EMIL HAAS, PHILIP HOHL, CARL HARTWIG, CHRISTIAN HAFNER, ERNST HAFENSACK, WILLIAM JORDAN, GEORGE JUNGINGER, CHARLES JUNG, HERMAN JOCHMUS, JOHN KRAUS, FRIEDRICK KIEHNE, ADOLPH KAUFMANN, CARL KOLB, JACOB KELSH, JACOB LEIER, THEODORE LOHR, GEORGE MERKLE, FELIX MICHAELKOWSKY, ALBERT MANN, AUGUST MARKOWSKY, ADOLPH NICKEL, LEONARD ROOS, FRANZ RECHT, CHARLES RITTER, ADOLPH REIMANN, CHARLES RICHTER, DAVID ROGALINA, CHARLES RAESER, EMIL STEEGE, ADOLPH SCHMIDT, JAMES SHAW, WILLIAM STARK, LOUIS SCHUMANN, NELSON STEINDECKER, VALENTINE SCHREINER, EDWARD SCHEUERMAN, CONRAD THONGS, WILLIAM THUMM, GEORGE THALMAN, HENRY WELLMAN, ADOLPH WEIS, JACOB WALKER, CONRAD WITTIG.

ALL PRESENT AND ACCOUNTED FOR!

As the two years went by, we witnessed many changes of our officers. Anthony Bracklin left us and went to the 45th New York Regiment. On August 2, 1861, he was replaced by William Syring, who stayed with us until November 3. Then, he followed Bracklin into the 45th New York Regiment. Subsequently, Henry Kluckhuhn, our First Speaker's brother, was appointed captain and remained as such until we were mustered out.

First Lieutenant Munich was transferred to Company I on April 21, 1862. George Koenig replaced him but was discharged on July 10, 1862. Alban Hottenroth, who was brought over from Company C to be our ensign and later promoted to the rank of first lieutenant, returned to Company C on September 18, 1862, the day after the battle at Antietam. He was replaced by Frederick Rosencrantz at the end of October, 1862. Rosencrantz held the first lieutenant's position until the end of our service.

Ensign Fritz Letzeiser, transferred to another company on August 6, 1861, and was replaced by Charles Lorch from Company G. Lorch was succeeded by Hottenroth, who, upon promotion to the rank of first lieutenant, was followed by Ferdinand Lange. Ferdinand's brother, William Lange, was appointed in his place on February 24, 1863 and remained as ensign until our muster-out.

Official records will show that Francis Weiss resigned on July 4, 1862; but, to my knowledge, he did not resign; he was a shirker of duty and dishonored himself in the Battle of White Oak Swamp by deserting. He was our colonel from April 28, 1862, until he disappeared from the regiment on June 30, 1862. Before the war I did not know very much about his background except that he was a good friend of Max Weber.

Weber, our regimental colonel from our enrollment date until he was promoted to the rank of brigadier general and replaced by Weiss, was born in Achern, Baden in 1824. He first studied at the Baden Polytechnic School. Later, he transferred to the Karlsruhe Military Academy and graduated in 1843. While he was a lieutenant in Duke Leopold's Baden Army, he was attracted to the philosophy of other Acht-und-vierziger like Franz Sigel, Friedrich Hecker, Karl Schurz, and Gustav Struve. He defected, along with his regiment, from Leopold's army, joined the revolutionists in 1848, and, for two years, fought under Mieroslowski and Sigel. He distinguished himself as an artillerist and was commissioned a colonel.

After the revolution was suppressed, he came to America, settled in New York City, and operated the Konstanz, a hotel at the corner of William and Franklin Streets. It was a rendezvous for German refugees and many of them, after being processed at Castle Garden, boarded there until they settled themselves in their adopted country. After Weber had organized the 20th New York Regiment, he was asked to incorporate it into Blenker's German Division. He refused.

Louis Blenker was another Acht-und-vierziger. He was born at Worms and was 12 years older than Weber. In 1848, he led his rebel force in battles in Baden and the Palatinate and captured Ludwigshafen, Worms, and Bobenheim. Near the end of the conflict, he was defending the town of Gernsbach against a Prussian siege. He continued the defense even though the struggle was already lost, and many women and children were sacrificed because of his stubbornness. Weber remembered this tragedy and never forgave Blenker. This may have been the reason why Weber refused to incorporate our regiment into Blenker's division.

Weber received his promotion to the rank of brigadier general on April 28, 1862. Following the promotion, he led the first wave in the attack on Norfolk, Virginia, in May, 1862. Late that summer he received command of the Third Brigade in the Third Division of the Second Army Corps, under General William H. French. At the battle of Antietam, he was severely wounded during an attack on the Sunken Road. Leading his men, he fought gallantly; and, while they took murderous fire, his right arm was shattered. For nearly a year he was confined to the hospital.

In 1864, he fought in the Shenandoah Valley under General Franz Sigel and General David Hunter; and, although he had only 800 men, he defended Harper's Ferry against Confederate General Jubal A. Early's raid in July, 1864. On August 20, 1864, he was given a 20 days leave of absence. His old wounds required additional medical attention. Upon return to active duty, he returned to Harper's Ferry and served under General John P. Stevenson. He resigned from the service on May 13, 1865. Subsequently, he was appointed American consul to Nantes, France. In 1870, at the beginning of the Franco-Prussian War, he returned to America. He accepted a position as tax assessor from the Department of Internal Revenue, and, upon appointment by President Ulysses S. Grant, he became tax collector in the department, covering the area of New York City and Long Island. At retirement in 1887, he moved to 458 Willoughby Avenue in Brooklyn and lived there 17 years until he died from lung disease on June 15, 1901. His wife had passed away eight years before; they had no children. At the time of his death he was a member of the Trinity Lodge of Masons, of Kolte's Post of the Grand Army of the Republic, and of the Liederkranz in Manhattan.

After our muster on Staten Island, we drilled daily at the Turnhalle and in Harmonie Garden. Later, we set up camp at Turtle Bay. On June 4, 1861, Weber received orders to have our regiment ready to sail to Fortress Monroe on June 13. The announcement was made while we hosted the New York City Council at Turtle Bay. At this ceremony, Frederick Kapp presented a sword to Colonel Weber saying, "A German soldier here has a double fame. He enlisted for his adopted country, and he has to do honor for the German name. The German stands foremost in the ranks of fighters for freedom."

Following this presentation, we passed in review, clad for the first time in our new uniforms. New York State had furnished the "basics" in the middle of May, and a committee of Turnschwestern provided "alterations." They supplied us with underclothing, blankets, bandages, ornamental accessories, and accouterments not provided by New York State. They designed for us a special truncated, conical hat with a wide brim furled on one side. Implanted on its front was a bugle, the symbol of the infantry, and the top was decorated with a green pompon. They also altered our frock coat and trousers, supplied by the State of New York. These garments were similar to the army's official issue, but the Turnschwestern added shoulder tabs, belt loops, and horizontal stripes on the cuffs. The stripes were green, as was the stripe which ran down each leg of our blue trousers. The welts and facings were also green, as were the stripes and chevrons of the non-commissioned officers and the shoulder straps of the officers. With these alterations, we were dressed in the fashion of a European rifleman, but we carried the oval "US" buckle on our waist belt.

That day, June 4, we carried the 720 percussion musket 1842; but, in July, we were issued the M-1840 Remington Mississippi rifle of 54 caliber. To it, we attached a Jager, which was a sword bayonet different from the angled bayonet of regular issue. Our cartridge boxes, box belts and plates, waist belts, cap pouches and picks, frogs for the swords, bayonet scabbards, gun slings, knapsacks, haversacks, canteens, and forage caps were supplied by the State of New York.

Kapp informed the Turner societies of our departure date. Immediately, they prepared for a massive celebration and distributed a published program to all those interested in extending farewell wishes to us. On June 13, 1861, many German societies were represented in the celebration. Among those present were: the Turnvereine, whose members were in the regiment, the New York Song Society, the Mozart Male Chorus, the Dramatic Club, the Arion Society, the Helvitia Male Chorus, and the New York Schuetzengilde. It was the largest celebration given to any German regiment leaving New York City during the Civil War.

The various groups gathered together at preassigned places on the morning of June 13. At two in the afternoon, the Turnvereine and the Schuetzengilde formed a procession and marched to City Hall. Members of the other groups went immediately to their assigned places. All patiently awaited our arrival.

Meanwhile, we broke camp at noon and proceeded to New York City. We were accompanied by the De Kalbe Zouaves, another German regiment. Together, we marched up Broadway. All streets and side streets were crammed with onlookers, who waved to us from doorways and windows. It was very exciting to march in our dress uniforms with the band playing and admirers throwing flowers from all directions. At five o'clock we arrived at City Hall. At the beginning of the ceremonies, the De Kalbe Zouaves' 45 piece band and drum corps filled the square with martial music. All present cheered!

Looking up, we saw a huge display of banners, badges, and mottoes. Behind the stage built in front of City Hall was the large Turner flag, featuring the ogling owl with a torch in one claw and a sword in the other. Under the owl, whose one eye winked amorously at us, were written the words, Gut Heil! Our regiment passed in review before the members of the assembled City Council. This review was followed by speeches and the presentation of flags. The Turnschwestern presented Colonel Weber with our regimental flag, which they had woven, and our First Speaker offered us the German tricolors: black, red, and gold. Upon completion of the ceremonies, with the band playing German melodies, the Vereine escorted our march to the docks on South Street, where we boarded the steamer *Alabama.*

That night, we set sail for Old Point Comfort, Virginia. There, in the months to follow, we were to be attached to the units stationed in and around Fortress Monroe. Fortress Monroe, the largest of all the installations at Old Point Comfort, guarded the mouth of the James River, commanded the entrance to Hampton Roads from the Chesapeake Bay, and was eleven miles from Norfolk. Shaped like a seven pointed star, it was surrounded by a water-filled moat eight feet deep, and in some places 150 feet wide. Construction of the fortress began in 1819, was completed in 1834, and covered about 282 acres.

We arrived on June 20 and disembarked. We marched to Tyler's Point on the north side of Mill Creek near the town of Hampton and set up our tents. Around us we found regiments from Massachusetts, New York, and Vermont. The compound, called Camp Hamilton, had come into existence out of necessity in 1861.

When the war began in April, 1861, Fortress Monroe was under the command of Colonel Justin Dimick of the Second U.S. Artillery. We celebrated with him his 61st birthday on August 5, 1861. On April 28, Colonel David W. Wardrop and Colonel Abner B. Packard reinforced Dimick's command with the 3rd and 4th Massachusetts Regiments. After their arrival, Dimick, who, at that time, was in constant communication with General-in-Chief Winfield Scott in Washington, informed the general that ammunition and 200,000 complete rations had arrived with Wardrop and Packard. He also thanked Scott for the increase to his command, which just prior to the new additions consisted of 1134 enlisted men and 73 officers, with ten sick in the infirmary and three confined to garrison for misconduct.

Around May 1, the 4th Massachusetts Regiment seized Villa Margaret, the summer home of former President Tyler. The regiment wanted to use the house as a barracks and prepare the surrounding area for the tents of those regiments which had arrived in April and those expected to arrive in May and June. Mrs. Tyler, formerly Julia Gardiner, when evicted by the Yankees, yelled at them, "You scum of the earth!" The bivouac area was first called Camp Troy; but later, with the inclusion of the Segar Farm, it was renamed Camp Hamilton in honor of the military secretary of General Winfield Scott. His secretary, Lieutenant Colonel Schuyler Hamilton, had been sent to Fortress Monroe to advise General Benjamin F. Butler, who outranked Dimick and took command on May 26, 1861.

When we arrived in June, Butler was the commander of all units. Colonel Dimick was placed in charge of the batteries within the fort and General Ebenezer W. Pierce was the commandant of the troops at Camp Hamilton. By the end of June, the entire complex was defended by 8,000 troops who patrolled and scouted much of the lower Peninsula to within a few miles of Big Bethal and Little Bethal.

During the last week in June, our regiment was introduced at Old Point Comfort with a formal inspection. For us, the day was a festive occasion, which was celebrated according to military fashion but catering to our German culture. The large veranda at headquarters was decorated with flowers and branches according to the custom of decorating in the towns and villages of Baden on state and religious holidays. At both ends of the veranda, the Stars and Stripes waved; the German tricolors, the Turner flag, and our regimental flag were also prominently displayed. In front of the veranda, we constructed a large stage with the surrounding space assigned for spectators.

At six o'clock in the afternoon, we stood in full dress, waiting inspection. Butler appeared on horseback accompanied by his wife and daughter, his staff, four other colonels, and many visitors. The other regiments stationed at Old Point Comfort were present including some from Camp Butler, which was located seven miles away at Newport News.

After inspection, Colonel Weber and his officers received the guests and escorted them to the veranda where they were served refreshments. On stage we performed the "Turner Exercises" as entertainment. Each of our companies did a specialty. Our company did tumbling exercises and Company C built a large human pyramid, using one half the unit. The guests rendered a thunderous applause. Butler was amazed at the poise, agility, and control of the Turners and publicly expressed himself in this regard. He was also pleased to see so many Bostonians, his former constituents, in Company G.

At twilight, the musical instruments were brought forth, and, during the evening, all were treated to German folk songs and music. After the concert, we met with friends from the 7th New York Regiment who, under the leadership of Colonel Bendix, had come to Old Point Comfort in June before we arrived.

After this celebration, we returned to camp and settled down to a life of obeying orders. General Benjamin F. Butler was a strict disciplinarian, forbidding any foraging, despoiling, and ravaging of the abandoned plantations on the lower tip of the Peninsula. We sometimes had difficulty in conforming to his regulations. The army mess was disgusting! We were accustomed to a meal of rye bread, wieners, pumpernickel, potato salad, cottage cheese, caraway-seed bread, sauerkraut, and sausage. The usual American meal was flat and tasteless at its best, but our first meals at Camp Hamilton were intolerable. Often, we complained to Captain Bracklin, but he told us to be patient. He said, "The problem could have been due to a lack of experience in the quartermaster corps; but, after some investigation, I know that we are being exploited by dishonest contractors."

Setting the food situation aside, we did have, with little reservation, much respect for our commander, General Benjamin Butler. He was a politician and a good organizer and manager. Before the war, he lived in Boston and prospered as a lawyer and investor. When he became sufficiently wealthy, he turned to politics as an outlet for his energy and became prominent in the Democratic Party. At the party's convention in Baltimore, June 23, 1860, he opposed the candidacy of Stephen Douglas for the presidency, and, subsequently, he joined the Southern Secessionist Democrats, helping them to campaign for John Cabel Breckinridge from Kentucky. The Southern Democrats split from the Northerners and held their own convention in Baltimore on June 28, 1860. Because of a lack of political loyalty, Butler was often considered to be led by egotism rather than ideology. He was bombastic and his decisions were sometimes considered reckless. In the winter of 1861, he advised the "lame duck," Buchanan, to have the South Carolina commissioners arrested and tried for treason. He argued, "It is the duty of the Supreme Court to determine their right of secession." Ironically, during this period, he was found consulting with several of his southern colleagues and was accused of being a traitor. A political mystery he was. A traitor he was not!

Following the surrender of Fort Sumter, April 13, 1861, Butler immediately activated his rank as brigadier general of the Massachusetts Militia. It was the only state in the Union immediately prepared, militarily, for the crisis. Within two days, he organized four regiments and offered them to Lincoln to forestall any Confederate advances. General Winfield Scott, general-in-chief of the United States Army, ordered him to send three regiments to the defense of Washington and a fourth to Fortress Monroe. The 6th Massachusetts Regiment was the first to go to Washington. It had to march through Baltimore because there was no rail connection between north Baltimore and the terminal of the Baltimore-Washington Railroad. The Baltimore and Ohio Railroad, from New York to Baltimore, ended at Relay House north of the city.

On their march, some troops were stoned by a rowdy crowd of southern sympathizers, and the regiment replied to the assault by firing into the crowd, killing and wounding civilians. Butler was shocked! He re-routed the other two regiments and advised General Scott to do the same with any other regiments coming down from the northeast. They were directed to go to Perryville, on the north shore of the Susquehanna River, take the steamer to Annapolis, and use rail transportation from there to Washington. The 6th Massachusetts Regiment arrived at the capital on April 19. Butler's other two regiments, along with the 7th New York Militia and a Rhode Island regiment, arrived on April 25.

Then, Butler was given command of the newly formed Department of Annapolis and immediately secured the defense of the capital. Subsequently, he took his 6th Massachusetts Regiment back to Baltimore, located artillery on Federal Hill, set up headquarters at the Relay House, subdued the secessionists, and effected a direct, unmolested troop movement to Washington.

In May, after these successes, he was informed by General Scott that he would be promoted to the rank of major general and placed in command of Fortress Monroe. Butler regarded this assignment as downgrading and unappreciative of his efforts. He raged, verbally but forcefully, against the War Department but eventually bowed to its wishes. He took command on May 26. Actually his protest was unnecessary because not only was he given command of Fortress Monroe, but he also assumed command of the newly formed Department of Virginia, which embraced an area of 60 miles around Old Point Comfort.

Immediately, upon his arrival, Butler formulated a set of objectives. Because he was determined not to allow the enemy to erect any batteries that could annoy Fortress Monroe, he sent troops out on skirmish to capture all enemy batteries within a half days march of the fortress. He also cooperated with the navy in attempts to recapture the navy yard near Portsmouth, Virginia, and destroy the batteries on Craney Island across Hampton Roads near Norfolk.

However, there were few expeditions and skirmishes on the Peninsula during the first part of July; and, in the few that did occur, our regiment was never engaged. The morale at Fortress Monroe and Camp Hamilton, justifiably or not, was very high. Prevalent was a great sense of security. Tourists, both male and female, still came to the Hygeia Hotel, which, since its erection in 1822, had been a renowned health resort with excellent bathing facilities. The hotel, in all its lavishness, was located near the main gate of the fort. Some families of the officers resided there, and the sutlers freely disposed of their wares in temporary shops that sprung up around the hotel.

Civilians as well as soldiers participated in ceremonial events which took place at Old Point Comfort during the summer of 1861. For them, the Fourth of July celebration was a full schedule of entertaining events. In the morning, the Stars and Stripes was raised while men, women, and children cheered, and the enlisted men threw their hats into the air. The regimental bands played vigorously. During the day, many orations were given. At Camp Hamilton, the entire regiment from Troy, New York sat on the ground in a large semi-circle and listened to their colonel, Joseph Carr, expound for one hour. The Union Coast Guard fired salutes from their field howitzers; and, in the evening, the troops, their families and friends, and even the Confederates in Norfolk were treated to a giant fireworks display, which was put on by the 5th New York Regiment. Along the walkways, our Turner regiment strung row upon row of candles, which were placed inside transparent globes, set up tables, and served beer, wine, cheese, and crackers. In the evening while our guests were eating and drinking, we entertained them with German folk songs. All had a joyous Gemuetlichkeit!

On July 24, discouraging war news from Washington put us on the alert. After the Union defeat at Bull Run, General Scott telegraphed Butler to send four regiments and long term volunteers to Washington. On July 26 and 27, the 3rd, 4th, and 5th New York Regiments and the 71st Pennsylvania Regiment left Camp Hamilton for the capital. The garrison at Fortress Monroe was so weakened that Butler abandoned his occupation of Hampton and ordered our forces back across the Hampton Creek Bridge. When Confederate General John B. Magruder learned of this, he sent 2,000 troops, under the command of Colonel Robert Johnston, to make a reconnaissance of Hampton and Newport News. However, they stayed in the area only a short time. Magruder realized that Fortress Monroe could not be taken by force. Hence, by July 30, the Confederates withdrew all their forces on the lower Peninsula back to Yorktown and Williamsburg.

On that day, we learned for the first time that an error had been made concerning our committed length of service. Although we thought that we had signed up for two years of service, we discovered that some of us were actually registered for only three months of duty. The confusion resulted because some New York State officals did not recognize the difference between the militia and the volunteer army and signed up five of our companies for three months and the other five companies for two years. Companies A through E wrongly belonged to the militia, and Companies F through K belonged to the volunteer army. The discrepancy was first recognized on July 10, 1861. On July 30, 1861, Simon Cameron, Secretary of War, requested Edwin D. Morgan, governor of New York, to rectify the situation. The same error had been made with the 12th, 13th, 19th, and 26th New York Regiments. Those members of our regiment involved in the discrepancy were given the choice to stay in the regiment or go home. The majority chose to stay. After much reflection I accepted the challenge to remain in the regiment for two years. I made my decision for the same reason I had made another decision on the Lombard Bridge in Hamburg seven years before. I wished to finish the work which I started out to do.

At Old Point Comfort, during July and August, John La Mountain was demonstrating for the Union Army the military value of his balloon invention. He ascended to 1,500 feet and, with his glass, scanned the terrain below. On one occasion, he made his ascent from land and went as high as 3,500 feet. On another occasion, he directed his ascent from the deck of the gunboat *Fanny*. This feat, on August 3, made the *Fanny* the first aircraft launcher in American history. In these ascents, La Mountain could survey a circular area of 30 mile radius. He discovered a concealed enemy camp at Sewell's Point, located another behind the Pig Point Battery, and observed the Confederate withdrawal to Yorktown.

It was unfortunate on the afternoon of August 6, when Magruder, again, advanced down the Peninsula to within a mile of the Newmarket Bridge, that La Mountain's vision was obscured. Magruder met no resistance and, with 4000 infantry, 400 cavalry, and a howitzer battalion, moved to the outskirts of Hampton. A copy of the *New York Tribune* had fallen into his hands. It, incorrectly, had notified the world that Butler had intended to occupy undefended Hampton, dispossess the inhabitants, and use the town as a camp for runaway slaves. Being angry, Magruder decided to destroy the colonial town and had it burned to the ground after cutting the telegraph line between Fortress Monroe and Newport News. Consequently, Butler was extremely angry with the *Tribune* and with the War Department that did not censure the newspaper.

Colonel Weber had made Butler aware of Magruder's anger. Weber had taken a patrol, consisting of units from the Turner Rifles, to New Market Bridge. Upon arriving, the Turners captured a man called Mayhew. He was a Rebel deserter, who swam across the creek and entered the Union camp. He was a native of Bangore, Maine, and, while serving as a commercial seaman, was captured by the Confederates. Subsequently, the Rebels compelled him to join a Georgia regiment called Baker's Fire Eaters. After his capture by Weber's men, Mayhew supplied the Union officers with much information concerning Magruder's movements and intentions.

After the burning of Hampton, Butler appealed to General Scott, forcefully and for the second time, having done so on June 29, requesting that a regular officer of rank and experience in the United States Army be sent to Fortress Monroe and take command. General John E. Wool, who was 78 years old and resided in Troy, New York, was asked to assume the command. He replied in the affirmative and arrived on August 17, 1861. He relieved Butler. Coincident with his taking the command, its title was changed to the Department of Southeastern Virginia. However, Butler remained at Old Point Comfort and was made commandant of Camp Hamilton. In this capacity, he assisted Wool. He directed the activities of the 1st, 2nd, 7th, 9th and 20th New York Regiments, a battalion of Massachusetts Volunteers, the Union Coast Guard, and a squadron of the First New York Mounted Rifles. While stepping down from his command of all the forces at Old Point Comfort, Butler especially praised the 20th New York Regiment for its uniform good conduct.

Previously, in June, 1861, while he was still in command of all the forces at Old Point Comfort, Butler had suggested a plan to conduct an amphibious assault on the Rebel defenses along the North Carolina coastline. At that time, the "army brass" dismissed his idea; but now Gideon Wells, Secretary of the Navy, after being advised by Captain R. D. Lowry, saw the wisdom in it. Wells gave his approval to Butler who, since he no longer commanded a department but was still eager to accept the challenge, explored his original idea further with Flag Officer Silas Stringham. The suggested plan had the ingredients of a spectacular command, one that could bring Butler coveted prestige. All through the war, he was adept at seizing good opportunities, and he was one of the few political generals who survived the war intact.

One day's sail south of Fortress Monroe lay the Outer Bank, the center of the North Carolina coastal region. It is a set of narrow, chain-like islands, approximately 200 miles long, shielding the North Carolina mainland. Inside the chain is the interlocking waterways' three sounds: Pamlico, Albemarle, and Currituck. Pamlico Sound, the largest of the three sounds, extends 90 miles from Roanoke Island in the north to the Neuse River in the south and has a maximum width of 40 miles. From Pamilco, by way of connecting rivers, Confederate ships could reach the cities of New Berne, Washington, Plymouth, and Winton in North Carolina. From the Albemarle, a canal connected these Outer Bank waterways, through Dismal Swamp, with Norfolk, Virginia.

Butler and Stringham realized the strategic importance of this coastal region. The Rebels also thought enough of its importance to initiate construction of fortifications along it. In early July, 1861, Federal vessels stood off shore, and their crews watched Rebel soldiers and slaves build forts and install cannons. At the end of July, 600 Confederate troops occupied these installations.

Through four inlets, ships could enter the "inland sea" from the Atlantic Ocean: Oregon in the north, Hatteras and Ocracoke in the center, and Beaufort in the south. The largest Rebel defenses were at Forts Macon, Hatteras, and Morgan. A Confederate fleet of four steamers, known as the mosquito fleet, patrolled the waterways between the forts and seized merchant ships along the coast. These were the *Winslow*, known in former years as the *Coffee*, the *Beaufort*, the *Raleigh*, and the *Ellis*. The *Winslow* was armed with a 32-pounder, smooth bore cannon, and a rifled gun. The other three carried only one rifled gun each, and this gun was manned by soldiers or farmers. Sometimes, the guns exploded prematurely or their fuses were found faulty. Theoretically, this fleet should not have been considered an adequate navy for such a strategic area, but it did marvelous duty. In one sixteen week period, quickly slipping through the inlets into the ocean, it surprised and captured 16 ships traveling from the West Indies to ports in the North. It gathered so much loot from Yankee shipping that it became more than a "scruple in the merchants' shoes"! Gideon Wells was flooded with complaints from those merchants. They voiced one cry, "Stop the piracy along the Outer Bank!" At this time, Wells was ripe to accept Butler's suggestion to take expedient action in these waters.

Butler and Stringham considered the Confederate defenses. Two forts guarded the Hatteras Inlet, Hatteras and Clark. Hatteras was situated 220 yards from the inlet, and its guns could sink any enemy ship coming through the channel. Its walls were constructed of sand sheathed by planks. These were driven into the ground, slanted against the breastwork, and covered with marsh grass. Its weaponry consisted of several 32-pounders, all smooth bore and of short range. Although they were very effective against low draft ships coming through the channel, these 32-pounders were unable to effectively repulse an oceanside bombardment. Clark, about 600 yards northeast of Hatteras, was smaller and closer to the ocean. Its artillery consisted of five 32-pounders and two rifled guns. These outposts were garrisoned with about 350 men from the 7th North Carolina Artillery Regiment.

Small villages were also scattered throughout the islands, and the inhabitants, called Islanders, occupied themselves mainly with fishing and sheep herding. About ten miles to the north of the forts was the village of Hatteras, located on the sound side of the island, with an excellent harbor. Opposite the village, on the ocean side, was a tall lighthouse, a landmark and beacon for all coastal shipping. Portsmouth, a larger village than Hatteras, was located at the Ocracoke Inlet near Fort Morgan. Many of the wives and families of the Confederate garrison were billeted there. However, I recall woefully, that the islands were inhabited with more geese, sea gulls, crabs, and mosquitoes than people, and there was no source of fresh water other than rain.

The Rebel command at the Outer Bank appeared to be well organized. Samuel Barron, commissioned by the Confederacy, was responsible for the defense of the entire coast of Virginia and North Carolina. When he was at the Outer Bank, he set up headquarters at Portsmouth. The artillery units at Hatteras and Clark were under the command of Major W.S.G. Andrews, but the troops of the garrison reported directly to Colonel William F. Martin.

Butler's plan for an amphibious assault on the islands was naive but acceptable to Simon Cameron, Secretary of War. After a combined force of army and navy would capture Hatteras and Clark, the forts would be destroyed and outmoded vessels, loaded with stones, would be sunk at the inlet, forming an impregnable barrier to all ships going in or out of Pamlico Sound. By this plan, the Outer Bank would not be occupied but abandoned. Butler was convinced that, when his plan was fulfilled, the Rebel navy would leave the Outer Bank and New Berne, Washington, Plymouth, and Winton would be cut off from receiving foreign supplies, which were being transported by rail from these cities to the troops in Virginia.

On August 9, 1861, Flag Officer Stringham received from the capital a confidential dispatch advising him to organize a naval fleet in preparation for the assault proposed by Butler. On August 17, 1861, Wool directed Butler to organize the detachment of troops that would assist our navy in the attack. Wool told Butler that he had asked General Scott for an attack force of 25,000 men but that Scott was "flabbergasted." He repeated Scott's words, "You can do the job with 800 men!" However, Butler was unconcerned. During the next week, he sent messages to Colonel Rush C. Hawkins, commander of the 9th New York Zouaves and Colonel Max Weber, commander of the Turner Rifles, requesting that they meet with him. The colonels responded in the affirmative and the meeting was held at Camp Hamilton. After the officers reviewed Butler's plan, they decided that four companies from each of their regiments would participate. Butler added, "And you will be assisted by a unit from the Union Coast Guard and a company from the Second U.S. Artillery."

Then Stringham proposed the fleet. The *Minnesota*, captained by Henry Van Brunt, would be Stringham's flagship. She would be accompanied by the *Wabash*, the *Pawnee*, the *Monticello*, the *Harriet Lane*, and the *Cumberland*. They had a combined fire power of 100 guns. The *Minnesota*, the *Wabash*, and the *Pawnee*, powered by steam, would form the core of the attack force. The *Monticello* and the *Harriet Lane* were small draft vessels and could be used to support troop landings. The *Cumberland*, the oldest sailing war vessel in our navy, was to act in support. This action would be the *Cumberland's* last offensive naval engagement. Upon completion of this mission, she was to be moored in Hampton Roads and perform defensive operations. For troop transports, Stringham knew that he could charter two steamers, the *Adelaide* and the *George Peabody*. Each of these vessels would take, in tow, stone-weighted hulks with surf boats lashed topside. He also included in the fleet the tug, *Fanny*, small but powerful; in rough surf, she could maneuver better than any of the other ships.

Soon, news of these preparations became more than grapevine gossip. On August 20, 1861, Weber told his captains of Companies A,B,C and D, to ready their men for the expedition. The next day Captain Syring, who had replaced Bracklin in our company, told Franz Munich to inform the sergeants. Finally, toward evening, we were informed that we would participate in the invasion.

In the meantime, Stringham checked with Naval Intelligence. He discovered that Daniel A. Campbell of Maine and Henry W. Penny of New York were knowledgeable of the defense installations at Hatteras and Clark. Their merchant vessels had been captured by the mosquito fleet while they were transporting merchandise to New York from the West Indies. While they were held prisoners by the Confederates at Hatteras Inlet, they saw at least 50 ships pass in and out of Pamlico Sound. They could describe, accurately, the forts' construction and armaments and emphasized that the ammunition was in short supply. Further, Campbell and Penny gave Stringham and Butler valuable information concerning the surf associated with the wind directions and the location of sand bars at the inlet.

Finally, the plans became a reality. We began boarding the *George Peabody* and the *Adelaide* on Monday, August 26. The total number of troops was 880. There were 500 from the 20th New York Regiment, 220 from the 9th New York Regiment, 100 from the Union Coast Guard, and 60 from the 2nd U.S. Artillery. Departure was scheduled for that evening. The frenzied gathering and loading of the ships did not go unnoticed by the enemy, stationed at lookouts near Norfolk. On Tuesday morning, after we sailed, a Confederate officer wired Henry Toole Clark of North Carolina, informing him of our departure on the previous evening. Clark, who had replaced John Willis Ellis as Governor of North Carolina, speculated that, because of our steaming south, we must be headed for the Carolinas.

During the night, the sea became quite rough, rough enough to make many troops seasick but not rough enough to do damage to the hulks or small ships. At 9:30 A.M., on August 27, we sighted the Hatteras lighthouse. By afternoon, we anchored off the inlet, lowered our surf boats into the water, and tied them to the hulks. After checking all weapons, ammunition, and supplies we rested, waiting instructions for the landing that was to take place the next day. I began to write a letter to my sister, Theresa, but I was unable to complete it until the battle was over.

That evening, a strategy meeting was held aboard the *Minnesota*. Stringham outlined his immediate plan. In the morning, we were to be set ashore three miles north of the forts; our landing would be protected by the *Harriet Lane* and the *Monticello*. If the enemy decided to come out of the forts and attack us, they could be easily shelled by these ships in such a way that sufficient ground would be between us and the shelling; the explosions would not harm our landing craft. Meanwhile, the *Minnesota*, the *Wabash*, and the *Pawnee* would continue to bombard the fortifications.

Stringham further described his novel naval attack plan, which had never been tried before. Instead of having his ships move in, anchor, and fire as had been the custom in our navy, he proposed to shoot on the run. He believed that the fort gunners would not be able to adjust rapidly and hit the moving targets. He realized that this tactic would be difficult for sailing vessels, but he was convinced that steamers could carry out the task. Therefore, for the initial series of attacks, he advised the captain of the *Cumberland* to lie off shore and lob arching shells into the forts while the other ships made their moving attack. The *Minnesota* would be the first to go in, followed by the *Wabash* and then the *Pawnee*. After passing the forts at close range, these ships were to turn, circle, and return.

When Stringham had completed his remarks, Butler described his plan for the infantry after it would be ashore. It was to proceed up the beach on the sound side and attack the forts "carrying" them by bayonet. This was an expression he frequently used to describe hand-to-hand combat if the situation required it. The infantry attack was to be supported by cannon fire from the Second U.S. Artillery, firing from behind the infantry but moving forward with the infantry. Hopefully, this tactic would keep the enemy confined within its breastworks.

While these plans were being discussed, Colonel Martin, on shore and using his glass, could see that the Union forces were formidable; he knew that his small garrison would need reinforcements. He sent a courier to Lieutenant Colonel Johnston, who was in command of Fort Morgan, near Portsmouth on the Ocracoke Inlet. Fort Morgan was about 18 miles from Hatteras and could be approached from Pamlico Sound. However, no sailing vessels or steamers were available and the courier had to go by small boat. He did not reach Fort Morgan until the next morning.

At daybreak, on August 28, the sailors made ready for the bombardment and we boarded our landing craft. At 10:30 A.M., the warships opened fire following Stringham's plan. The shore batteries returned the fire; but, even with elevation for maximum distance, they could not reach our ships. The *Minnesota*, the *Wabash*, and the *Pawnee* delivered broadside after broadside. During this bombardment, the *Susquehanna*, returning from a tour of duty in the West Indies, sighted the fleet in action, and joined in the fight. She followed the direction of the *Minnesota*, and took her place in the attack formation. At one point in the attack, the smoke was so dense that the gunners were unable to see the forts. The Rebels were shocked as timber and sand were sucked into the air and splashed down again to the ground.

Up the shoreline, our landing party was in trouble. A strong southerly wind was blowing in toward shore off the ocean, the surf was running very high, and our landing craft were being caught by the breakers and hurled into shore. The small wooden boats were broken up and sank. Many troops were falling into the water, and much equipment was lost. Some members of our company, along with some troops from Company D, transferred to one of the two large hulks, and several soldiers from Companies A and C were in the other hulk. The Union Coast Guard was operating the hulks and the Second U.S. Artillery was loading cannon aboard. Many members of the 9th New York Regiment were in the water, hanging on to the sides of our hulk. We pulled them aboard. We threw out a cable, with an anchor on one end and with the other end fastened to the windlass. As the sailors continuously let out more line, our craft slowly drifted toward shore.

We were halfway to the beach, when the wind shifted to the East, and our situation became more dangerous. Waves broke over the sides of the hulks and drenched us. The cannons, lashed to the sides, almost broke loose. If the ropes had split, we would have been crushed! As it was, several of our men suffered cuts and bruises. When all seemed to be lost, the *Fanny* came between the two hulks and attached her lines to us. With her bow into the waves and her strong engines keeping her stationary in the water, she stabilized our condition. Gradually, she eased us through the waves to shallow water. As soon as possible, we evacuated the hulks and waded to the beach.

On the beach, after heads were counted, we discovered that 318 men had made it safely to shore. They made up a motley group, which contained 102 Turners, 68 Zouaves, 45 artillerymen, 45 marines from the *Minnesota*, 28 from the Union Coast Guard, and 28 sailors. Colonel Weber was in command of the landing party. Colonel Hawkins and the bulk of his regiment did not make it to the beach. Butler, aboard the *Harriet Lane*, when he saw the difficulty we were having, ordered the Zouaves and the remainder of our regiment to remain on the ships.

Besides Colonel Weber, the officers on shore from the 20th New York Regiment were Lieutenant Colonel Weiss, Captain von Doehn, Captain Hoeffling, Captain Meyers, and Adjutant Kluckhuhn. Captain Larned and Lieutenant Lodor were in command of the men from the 2nd U.S. Artillery. Captain Nixon directed the small force of Union Coast Guard, and Captain Jardine was in charge of the Zouaves. Lieutenant Wiegel, an ordnance officer of General Butler's staff, was also present.

Once we were ashore our real troubles began. We were wet to our shoulders, we had wet ammunition, we had no provisions, and we were informed that there would be no reinforcements. Fortunately, the *Harriet Lane* and the *Monticello* were nearby at sea and Colonel Weber assured us that their guns had the range to protect us until our ammunition dried and the artillery unit could become operational.

Suddenly, from the direction of the forts we saw a cloud of dust coming our way. It looked as if the Rebels were sending out a cavalry unit to pounce on us. The crew of the *Harriet Lane* opened fire, laying down quite an impressive barrage in front of the cloud, but it continued to come on. Colonel Weber, using his glass, reported excitedly, "It is a detachment of horse descending upon us! It is riderless!" Relieved, we discovered that it was a herd of terrified beach ponies seeking safety from the bombardment which our ships was savagely pouring onto Hatteras and Clark. When the herd passed by, some curious Islanders came out to investigate. They had been watching our boats struggle in the water and now wanted to get a closer look at the strange invaders. Coming close, the Islanders were treated to a new experience. Never before had they heard profanity spoken in German; and, under the circumstances, we were quite vocal!

We began to move down the shoreline. Colonel Weber sent Weiss and 20 Turners ahead of the main body to make a reconnaissance of Fort Clark. Soon we discovered that our situation was not so bad as first envisioned. The cannons from Clark were not firing. The Rebels had run out of ammunition, and Colonel Lamb ordered his men to spike the guns and evacuate. About one o'clock, we came within musket range of the fort and saw the Confederates running across the narrow causeway which separated Clark from Hatteras. Shells from our ships were bursting all around the Rebels and several were cut off, killed, or wounded. However, we did not enter the fort until we were reinforced by more troops from the 20th New York Regiment led by Captain von Doehn and Captain Heffling.

As we entered the fort, we could see that there was no flag flying from the staff at Hatteras. Butler, aboard the *Harriet Lane*, must have observed the same phenomenon and signaled the *Minnesota* to cease fire. He questioned, "Are the Rebels surrendering?" They were not! Their flag had been torn away by the wind after it had been shredded by our fleet's cannon fire. During this short period of cease fire, Stringham sent the *Cumberland* out to sea and ordered the *Monticello* to enter the channel and seize the fort. When she came within range, she was blasted with a broadside and her captain immediately sounded a retreat. She was struck several times; but, in about 50 minutes, she was again out of range. This miscalculation convinced Stringham that no surrender was being considered, and he recommenced the shelling with more force than before.

We were in the process of raising the Stars and Stripes over Clark when Stringham gave the order. Suddenly, his stray shells began exploding around us. We thought it ironic; we had weathered the waves only to be struck down by our own shells while raising the national flag. We quickly withdrew from the fort and took up positions of safety. Fortunately, only one man was slightly wounded, but our flag was flying above an empty fort.

Darkness and threatening weather caused Stringham to order a cease fire for the day. He ordered the larger vessels out to sea, but he allowed the *Harriet Lane*, the *Pawnee*, and the *Monticello* to move closer to shore behind Clark in order to protect our position. However, they could not remain there since the winds had increased, and a storm began to roll in. The ships moved out to deeper water; we were left to the mercy of the enemy and to our inventive tactics, by which we hoped to avoid being subdued and captured.

At dusk the *Winslow* and the *Ellis* arrived from Portsmouth with Rebel reinforcements. Samuel Barron came with them. He had been notified by Governor Clark of the message from Norfolk and was in Portsmouth when the courier arrived from Hatteras. Within a few minutes, he realized the seriousness of the Confederate situation. He found the troops who had sustained the day's bombardment exhausted. Colonel Martin was utterly prostrate. He asked Barron to take command. Barron did so and called a meeting of the officers, explaining that he expected more reinforcements from New Berne before midnight. With their arrival, he planned to attack us and recapture Clark. Midnight came, but no reinforcements arrived. Consequently, Barron and his officers agreed not to attack our positions. They had 800 men and we had only 318, but they were unaware of this difference. So, within 600 yards of our advanced position, they rested, ate food, and drank coffee.

For us the situation was different. We had no coffee and food and we could not rest! Colonel Weber prepared for the worst. He posted pickets. The Zouaves, under the command of Captain Jardine, were deployed on the beach approaching the outer breastwork of Hatteras and Captain Nixon, with 28 men from the Union Coast Guard, occupied Fort Clark. The main body of the troops withdrew to our landing site. When they were in position, they lit several camp fires so as to make our numbers appear greater than they were. We suffered from thirst, but we had no water to quench it. Some of our men scraped holes in the sand, but they found only brackish, distasteful, nauseous water. Others seized some sheep and geese, spitted them on their bayonets, and roasted them over the camp fire. The winds increased, the weather grew more foul, but no rain fell. If an attack had come, we would have had little accuracy in firing; we passed the night fearfully but protected by circumstance and nature.

The winds abated about 5:30 A.M. Immediately, the fleet weighed anchor and moved toward shore. At 7:30 A.M., the *Minnesota* signaled for the attack. For three hours and 20 minutes, a terrifying and horrendous shelling continued unabated with 1000 shells per hour focused on one small fort. The sound and sight were most frightful, but we were, thank God, not on the receiving end of it.

We watched our fleet in action. We saw a magnificent sight as the *Cumberland* went into battle under sail. Now, Stringham was allowing her captain to perform the standard naval attack strategem developed for sailing vessels. As she led the line of warships in toward shore, she would simultaneously shorten and furl her sails, throw in the anchor, and fire. Then quickly, she would hoist anchor, unfurl, and move out to sea. Over and over again, she patiently repeated this performance. It was an inspiring piece of seamanship, a tribute to her last offensive battle.

However, we were not spectators only. Again, we were inside the walls of Fort Clark, reinforcing the Union Coast Guard. Just before 11 A.M., someone ordered a cease fire. Presumably, Barron did not wish to continue the defense since his men could hardly raise their heads much less return any fire. He decided to spike the cannons and make a retreat. As he was composing the order, an unspent shell exploded in the ventilator and started a fire in the room next to the magazine. If that room exploded, all would be lost. He could not delay; and, as the fire was being extinguished, he ran up the white flag. Shouts of victory rang out on our ships and through our ranks on shore.

Quickly, the *Fanny*, with Butler aboard, approached the beach near the inlet. She weighed anchor and one of Butler's aides came ashore to discuss terms of surrender. Barron suggested that his officers be allowed to leave the fort with their side arms and the enlisted men be evacuated without weapons. Butler refused these terms. He called for complete surrender; all officers and men were to be taken prisoners. Butler extended this message to Barron by way of his aide and nervously awaited his reply. He had reason to be anxious. The *Adelaide*, loaded with the Zouaves and the rest of the artillery, had run aground. The *Harriet Lane*, trying to assist her, fell into the same trap. Both vessels were in range of the fort's guns, and their situation would be disastrous if the Rebels decided to continue the fight. Butler waited 45 minutes, during which the *Winslow* and the *Ellis* slipped away through Pamlico Sound carrying about 200 troops.

Finally, Barron signaled the *Fanny*, accepting the Federal terms. General Butler came ashore, and Captain Meyers and Adjutant Kluckhuhn led the Turners across the causeway to occupy Hatteras. However, the main body of troops remained about 50 yards outside the walls as Butler, Weber, Weiss, von Doehn, Nixon, and a small color guard entered. Inside the fort, the color guard raised the Stars and Stripes and displayed our regimental colors. Barron, Martin, Andrews, Lamb, and the other officers were taken aboard the *Minnesota*. The enlisted men were assigned to the *George Peabody*. We took 700 prisoners. In the two days of shelling, 15 Rebels were killed and 35 more were wounded. We had no fatal casualties and only one was wounded. The wounded Confederates were attended to by Doctor Hauser of the 20th New York Regiment, Doctor Humphreys of the 9th New York Regiment, and Doctor King of the United States Navy. Along with the prisoners, we captured 1000 rifles and 35 cannons. Subsequently, the prisoners were taken to Fortress Monroe and then to New York.

Without delay on Friday, Stringham with his Federal fleet sailed for Old Point Comfort. However, he left behind the *Pawnee*, the *Susquehanna*, the *Fanny*, and the grounded *Adelaide*. Butler accompanied the Federal fleet, but he ordered the Turners and the Zouaves to remain and garrison the forts. He placed Rush Hawkins in command of the occupation. His choice of Hawkins instead of Weber, both having equal rank, indicated to us the discrimination which existed in the military between the native Americans and the foreign born.

That Friday, August 30, 1861, was the 30th anniversary of my birthday. I completed my letter to Theresa which I began on August 27. I told her that I was excited and enjoyed celebrating, with my comrades, my birthday and the victory we had just achieved. It was the Federals' first major victory of the war. It was their first naval victory, and it was accomplished by Stringham's using for the first time his moving, hitting, and running tactics. It was the Federals' first amphibious landing and the first invasion of North Carolina. Pride was unavoidable! Our Turners had helped to bring the conflict, early in the war, directly into Confederate territory. We were the first to raise the Stars and Stripes in North Carolina. It was a special joy to see the German tricolors and our regimental flag waving beside our adopted country's flag. Ending my letter, I asked Theresa to pray that God would protect me and my comrades and see us through all future battles as kindly as He had this one.

Butler's original plan was not pursued. Ships were not sunk at the inlets and troops were not evacuated from the forts. The War Department considered it better and wiser to establish physical presence at the Outer Bank. Cameron telegraphed General Wool to hold the position at Fort Hatteras and take measures to effect a workable occupation. The Federals now had a foothold in North Carolina, one which gave them access to a great inland sea. It was also conceivable that, with Federal presence in the area, the local citizenry, who were not entrenched in the Confederacy, might support the Union cause.

Regretfully, on August 30, we began our occupation. It was not pleasant! We had been led to believe that three Rebel schooners, anchored inside the inlet, were laden with provisions; but, on investigation, we found only some fruits which were in the late stages of decay. Colonel Weber said, "You cannot eat those fruits. You will have to be satisfied with fish, if you catch them, black coffee, and pancakes." Ah! Such delightful pancakes! They were made of flour and salt water, and they were so hard that we called them sheet-iron! Then, Weber continued, "You will have to be content with this fare for ten days but relief will come." To this we replied, "Gut Heil!"

Each day we would go out in small boats and hunt for wild geese or fish in the sound. Crabs were plentiful as well as oysters. Sometimes, we would capture a large turtle. However, we were always in search of fresh water. After a few days, the Islanders complained to Hawkins that we were stealing from them, and they asked for remuneration. He and Weber had some heated debates over these complaints. In one burst of temper, Hawkins shouted at Weber, "If the plundering does not stop, I will use my artillery on the Turners as they are getting into their boats." Weber corrected Hawkins, "My men are dispatched to get water, firewood, and cooking apparatus. What meat they find is purchased, not stolen. Furthermore, I do not think that you are handling this situation in a proper military manner!"

Both men wrote their side of the incident to General Wool; but, on September 10, Lieutenant Betts, who was dispatched from Fortress Monroe under special orders from Wool, arrived with six more companies from Hawkins' 9th New York Regiment. He informed Hawkins that, on September 14, seven more companies from his Zouave Regiment would arrive. Further, he stated that these would be accompanied by some companies from the 20th Indiana Regiment. Then, Betts informed Weber that our regiment was ordered by Wool to return on the steamer *Spaulding* to Fortress Monroe on Septeber 12. Weber was furious! He was convinced that Wool had sided with Hawkins and the order for our removal was motivated by the Turners' alleged thievery and insubordination.

It was true that, on the night of our victory, after the other troops aboard the ships had come ashore, soldiers looted the abandoned Confederate camps. Our regiment and some of our officers were involved, but we were not alone in the fracas. The Zouaves were equally active. The situation got out of hand. It seemed as if the two regiments were in competition, the victory going to the regiment which could gain the most loot. Trunks were broken open, tents carried off, stoves snatched, and cooking utensils and food taken. Hawkins claimed he saw the Turners return to their camp sites with their arms full. He did not mention that he saw his Zouaves return with abundant booty. His eyes were probably closed as they passed by him. The accusations of the Islanders, such as our breaking into private homes and the burning of buildings, were falsely made. Hawkins should not have believed these accusations to be true. In reality, we were victims of Hawkins' jealousy. Recall, it was the German tricolors and our regimental flag which had been seen in victory before Hawkins was able to disembark from the grounded *Adelaide*.

If Weber felt bad, the enlisted men didn't. I would think myself to be insane if I were to have preferred the Outer Bank to the comfort of Camp Hamilton. Also, my experience during the last days of August and those first 12 days of September gave me sufficient fill of war for a time. My greatest joy that month resulted from receiving a letter from Francesca. She and George had returned from Europe and were adjusting to the war economy at their home in Philadelphia. She informed me that while they were in Forchheim, she became pregnant and carried the little one within her as they returned to America. She also told me of her sadness as they left the village. My mother had said to her, "I believe this will be the last time we shall ever see each other!" Francesca tried to assure her that, if it were God's Will, she and George would return.

During the remainder of the year 1861, our regiment focused its attention on activities around Old Point Comfort. A tremendous storm hit the Virginia coast on October 2. Mill Creek overflowed its bank and our camp was inundated with water the next day. We forgot the enemy as we turned to cleaning up the mess left in the wake of the flood. Through the remainder of October, we were kept close to camp and did not venture any further than the Hampton Creek Bridge. However, on November 11, we were sent north and were engaged in a skirmish with Rebel pickets at Sinclair's Farm. Again, on December 22, we fought a short battle with them at Back River Creek; both engagements were of little consequence.

By the end of December, Camp Hamilton had 5,427 troops bivouacked and General Wool had, under his command at the Old Point Comfort complex, 13,013 enlisted men and officers. Colonel Weber replaced General Mansfield as commandant of Camp Hamilton on November 23, 1861. Mansfield was sent to relieve General Phelps at Newport News. It was Wool's way of showing Weber that he did not completely believe the stories he had heard concerning the Turners' alleged conduct at the Outer Bank. As commandant, Weber had seven regiments under his command: the 1st Delaware, 16th Massachusetts, 20th Indiana, 20th New York, 99th New York, 11th Pennsylvania, and 1st New York Mounted Rifles.

Wool had been enlightened about the Islanders at the Outer Bank. He discovered that they were natural thieves and pirates. At night, these Islanders would hang lanterns from the necks of the beach ponies as the ponies wandered along the shore. Ships' captains, seeing the flickering lights, would assume other vessels to be nearby. In following the bobbing lights, the captains would turn toward shore and run aground. Subsequently, the ships were crushed by the pounding waves. Then, the island pirates, pretending to offer aid to the troubled crews, looted the disabled ships. A particular group of Islanders, called Buffaloes, claimed to be Union sympathizers, ready to fight for the cause. They did no fighting but confined their activities to robbery and pillage of their neighbors. Following one of their raids in which they wore disguises, they encouraged their victims to seek compensation from the Union officers who were in charge of the occupation forces.

The new year brought renewed military activity to Fortress Monroe. On January 3, 1862, Lieutenant Colonel Weiss led six companies of the Turner Rifles on a reconnaissance of Big Bethal, Virginia. He was also accompanied by three companies of the 11th Pennsylvania Cavalry under the command of Colonel Spears and units of the Union Coast Guard led by Colonel Wardrop. The task force left Camp Hamilton at 9 AM and reached Big Bethal at 10 AM. It engaged the Rebels and routed them. Weiss made a survey of the fortifications and found that the redoubts built by the Rebels could accommodate about 3000 men. After the survey, Weiss led his men back to Camp Hamilton. Upon arrival, he immediately reported to Colonel Weber and said, "Our mission was a success. On our return, we found all the farm houses and barns burned or destroyed. The whole countryside presents a sad picture of desolation."

On January 10, 1862, we witnessed the troops of the Burnside expedition rendezvous at Old Point Comfort. Eighty ships assembled in the harbor. One night, with the ships illuminated, it looked like a festive occasion; bands were playing martial music while troops were boarding. General Ambrose Burnside had been assigned to lead a division of 15,000 men against the coastal region of North Carolina. By the end of February, he occupied Roanoke Island. By March, the Confederates evacuated New Berne. Subsequently, Forts Macon and Beaufort surrendered. On July 3, 1862, final success of the operation was announced. Following these successes, Burnside was recalled and placed in command of the Ninth Corps of the Army of the Potomac. Describing his North Carolina expedition, he said, "It was a succession of honorable victories!" All the areas that he occupied during his command at the Outer Bank remained in Federal hands for the duration of the war. However, I never forgot that it was our Turner regiment that first invaded the state.

With the exception of engaging the enemy at New Market Bridge, on January 22, 1862, we had no other skirmish experience during the winter of that year. On April 28, Colonel Weber was promoted to the rank of brigadier general and given a command in the Seventh Corps when it was formed. At this time, I considered our first year of war to have ended. We had served almost 12 months and we could feel that our long stay at Old Point Comfort was about to be terminated. I wrote to my parents on May 1, 1862. I expressed great fear of the future. I longed to be back in New York painting with Enrico Tassi. War! Its novelty and its luster were beginning to grow old and dim!

Left: General William F. Smith. On May 9, 1861, he performed the muster ceremony of the 20th New York regiment on Staten Island. Right: A uniformed Turner soldier dressed in the fashion of a European rifleman.

Officers of the 20th New York Regiment (United Turner Rifles). The photograph was taken in New York City prior to the regiment's leaving for camp at Turtle Bay. Regulation uniforms with approved alterations of the Turnschwestern had not been issued. The uniforms shown were supplied by the photographer.

Max Weber. Colonel and leader of the 20th New York Regiment from May 9, 1861 to April 28, 1862. He rose to the rank of brigadier general and was severely wounded at Antietam, September 17, 1862.

Left: Ernst Mattais Peter von Vegesack. Colonel of the 20th New York regiment from July 19, 1862 to June 3, 1863. He brought the regiment to glory at Antietam. Right: Francis Weiss. Colonel of the 20th New York Regiment from April 28, 1862 to July 4, 1862. He brought humiliation to the regiment at White Oak Swamp.

Maj. Gen. Benjamin Butler
22 May, 1861 to 17 August, 1861.

Maj. Gen. John E. Wool
17 August, 1861 to 2 June, 1862.

COMMANDING OFFICERS AT FORTRESS MONROE.

Independence Day celebration at Fortress Monroe, 1861. Originally, the sketch appeared in Harper's Weekly, 27 July, 1861. The 20th New York Regiment (Turner Rifles) is featured in the upper right under the title "Illumination."

Hampton Roads and vicinity. The 20th New York Regiment did duty in this region during its first year of war.

Scenes at Old Point Comfort, 1861

Upper Left: Camp Hamilton seen from Fortress Monroe. Upper Right: Fortress Monroe with the Hygeia Hotel in the foreground (both drawn by E. Sachse). Lower Left: Turners during flood of October 3, 1861. Lower Right: Colonel Max Weber's headquarters. Turners in foreground (both drawn by H. Sartorious).

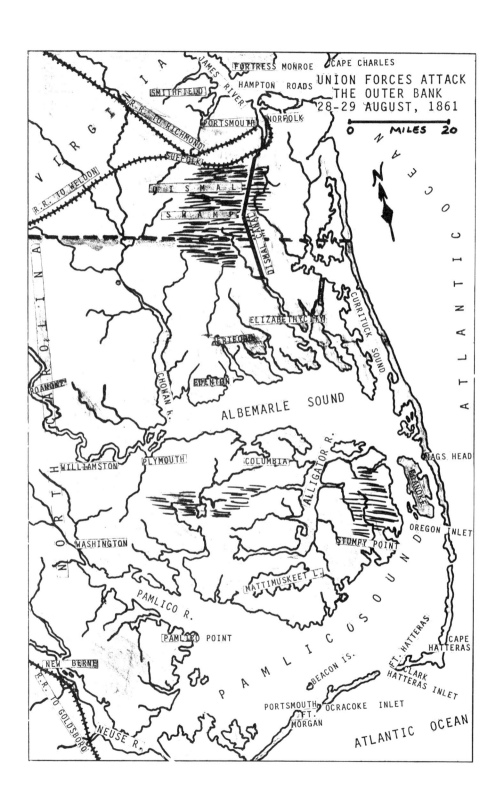

Landing at Hatteras Inlet. A motley group made it safely to shore: 102 Turners, 68 Zouaves, 45 artillerymen, 28 Union Coast Guard, and 28 sailors. Sketch by A.R. Waud.

Opposing naval officers at Hatteras Inlet, 28-29 August, 1861. Left: Silas Stringham (Union), and Right: Samuel Barron (Confederate).

THE SOLDIERS WE WERE TRAINED TO BE

The year 1862 was climactic for me. That year, our regiment experienced pain, humiliation, and glory associated with fierce combat. In the spring, our physical fitness was excellent, and we had been well trained by Colonel Weber in the best methods of European drill; but, actually, we were untried soldiers. Except for the members of our four companies who had gone to Hatteras Inlet, very few other men in our regiment had heard the roar of cannons or seen the bursting of shells. After ten months of service, not one of us had made an attack against a concentration of artillery, attempting to penetrate its destructive power. However, we were proficient using our muskets. We could load, ram, and fire at least two rounds per minute. We could also use the bayonet proficiently, wheel right and wheel left, fire in ranks, infiltrate enemy lines, and march double-quick for long distances; but, as to doing these things under combat conditions, we were greener than the stripes on our trousers.

On May 9 and 10, 1862, we were part of the amphibious force that landed at Willoughby's Point and attacked Norfolk; but, really, this was a skirmish rather than hard combat. On June 13, we arrived at the front on the Chickahominy River, where McClellan was planning his attack on Richmond. From that day until September 18, we knew little rest. During that span of time, we maneuvered from Fortress Monroe to Sharpsburg, Maryland and engaged the enemy at Chickahominy River, Savage's Station, White Oak Swamp, Malvern Hill, South Mountain, and Antietam Creek. When we emerged from this series of battles, our German tricolors took on new meaning: black for our betrayal and humiliation; red for our blood shed on the battlefield; and gold for the glory we achieved, becoming the soldiers we were trained to be! In order to appreciate our regiment's rise from well trained but "green" combat soldiers to a fighting unit which could forever be proud of its achievements, I must start with events which took place far away from our camp at Old Point Comfort.

After the battle of Bull Run, in July, 1861, the Union army returned to Washington demoralized. Congress demanded the removal of General Irvin McDowell from command of the Department of Northeastern Virginia. Lincoln agreed. In his place, he appointed George B. McClellan, a West Point graduate, who had served in the Mexican War. McClellan had attained the rank of captain but resigned from the army in 1857 at the age of 37. At the outbreak of the Civil War, he was employed by the Illinois Central Railroad as vice president. Quickly, he was recalled into the army and given the rank of major general.

In the early months of the war, he conducted successful campaigns in western Virginia. Lincoln was well aware of his organizational skills, having done legal service for the Illinois Central while McClellan was vice president. Now, the army, mainly a volunteer one, needed organization. Staff departments and staff officers were to be fashioned out of intelligent and enthusiastic but perfectly raw material. Artillery, smallarms, and ammunition were to be fabricated or purchased from abroad; wagons, ambulances, bridge trains, camp equipment, hospital stores, and the vast impedimenta indispensable for an army in the field were to be manufactured and deployed. McClellan had the ability and desire to implement these requirements.

In late summer, McClellan came to Washington and took command of all forces in and around the capital. He began to build his powerful fighting machine! Congress, before adjourning in August, voted the men and money he would need and led him to believe that he would be in charge of 300,000 men. As he took to the task with vigor, they referred to him as the young Napoleon.

In the fall of 1861, he portrayed himself as an officer in the saddle. He was highly visible on the avenues of the capital as he labored to establish himself before building the army. He gathered West Point graduates around him and gave them key positions and promotions. In the months that lay ahead, when newspapers would report victory and defeat, the populace would read the names of his appointees: Heintzelman, Franklin, Kearny, Porter, Meade, Hooker, Sedgwick, Hancock, Reynolds, Keyes, Sumner, and Smith.

Although McClellan favored visits to camps of foreign troops, like Blenker's German Division, he was not prone to select immigrants for positions higher than that of colonel. A few of his high ranking officers were heard to say, "McClellan's army will be led by regulars; those non-English speaking immigrants will make good men of the ranks and carry the burden of defeat. But, will we let them share in the glories of victory?" However, Blenker was promoted to the rank of brigadier general of volunteers, and McClellan did revel in aristocratic shoulder rubbing with foreigners such as those at Blenker's headquarters. One night in November, 1861, two thousand of Blenker's troops, dressed in European uniforms, participated in a special procession conducted for McClellan. The ceremony ended with a fantastic fireworks display.

Furthermore, many foreign military visitors and knights- errant were graciously welcomed as aides-de-camp at McClellan's headquarters. However, some members of his staff disliked their presence. One regular army officer, humorously but sarcastically, remarked, "So many veterans of the Crimea are jostling shoulders with the Garabaldians in the hallways of Willard's that it is almost impossible for me to find a path to my room!" McClellan made Louis Philippe d'Orleans, the Comte de Paris, the pretender to the throne of France, and his brother, Robert d'Orleans, Duc de Chartres, aides-de-camp and gave each of them the rank of captain in the Union army. They had been exiled, during the reign of Napoleon III and came to America to observe the war and study military tactics. During their stay, they were chaperoned by their uncle, the Prince de Joinville. He held no rank in the army, but his son was attending the United States Naval Academy, which had been moved from Annapolis to Newport in Connecticut.

By the end of November, McClellan had about 175,000 men under his command. He called them the Army of the Potomac. As he grew in importance he also grew in arrogance and treated General Winfield Scott, our general-in-chief, with contempt. Scott complained, "Four years ago he was only a captain, and now he treats me like a subordinate!" Finally, Scott could no longer stand the young Napoleon's snobbery and retired. Then, Lincoln wondered if McClellan could take over the duties of the retired general-in-chief but worried that it might be impossible for him to handle that job plus being active commander of the Army of the Potomac. He asked him, "Is this too much for one man?" McClellan responded, "I can do it all!"

Once McClellan accepted both positions, organization, training, grand parades, and reorganization of the Army of the Potomac followed; but, no battles! Lincoln became depressed. He thought, "McClellan must have the wrong priorities; surely, he doesn't have mine." Sardonically, the *Daily Telegraph* announced, "All's quiet on the Potomac!" It was so quiet that the French princes who had become McClellan's aides-de-camp planned an excursion to Niagara Falls.

In December, McClellan disappeared from public view. The newspapers claimed that he had a cold and was confined to his private quarters on H Street in Washington. After Christmas, they changed their "diagnosis." They reported his having typhoid but hinted that, from his sick bed, he was planning the siege of Richmond. Members of the War Department tried to find out his plans, but he refused to confide in them. They begged of him, "Please confide in Mr. Lincoln, if not in us." He replied, "I will not! If I tell him something today, I will read it in the *New York Tribune* tomorrow morning." Edwin McMasters Stanton, who had replaced Simon Chase as Secretary of War, was furious with his remark.

January and February faded into history. The Army of the Potomac remained encamped in and around the capital, and the officers enjoyed the night life and social gatherings at Willard's and the other hotels in Washington. Lincoln complained to Stanton, "The Army of the Potomac dawdles around Washington, polishing buttons and stirrups, while Grant, Sherman, and Thomas are battling and succeeding in the West, and reports of Burnside's victories in North Carolina are making headlines." Stanton replied, "McClellan was right; he can do it all because he does nothing!"

On February 22, Lincoln reached the end of his patience. The First Congress of the Confederate States of America had met on February 18 and officially inaugurated Jefferson Davis as their president. The North was now at war with a "new nation." Lincoln worried, "Foreign intervention in this conflict is now imminent; and, if we show no military prowess, the political situation will be disastrous. McClellan must be removed from the post of general-in-chief."

After McClellan's removal, Stanton assumed his duties until a new military man could be appointed. Stanton acted quickly and without McClellan's knowledge. On March 11, he broke the army up into four corps and assigned officers to each. McClellan was allowed to keep about 145,000 troops and was ordered by Stanton to proceed with his plans to capture Richmond. These called for an invasion of the Peninsula, followed by the occupation of Yorktown and Williamsburg, and a direct assault on Richmond after the crossing of the Chickahominy River. Preparations were immediately made by McClellan to move his troops from the capital to Fortress Monroe and use it as a springboard for his invasion.

Two days before these events took place, a dramatic and world shocking naval battle had been completed in Hampton Roads outside the range of Fortress Monroe's cannons. It was a battle the result of which influenced McClellan's invasion plans. Also, it was an event which changed the naval strategy of the war.

In the spring of 1861, Norfolk and the navy yard at Portsmouth, Virginia, had been hurriedly abandoned by the Federals and, in the Federals' haste to leave, they left 1,200 heavy guns intact but scuttled the ships. The Confederates installed the cannons on gunboats and in forts stretching from the Potomac to the Mississippi River and salvaged the ships. One of the frigates scuttled was the *Merrimac*, a sister ship to the *Minnesota* and the *Roanoke*. During the fall and winter, the Rebels raised her hull, cut her down to the berth deck, reinstalled her 40 guns, rebuilt the midsection with 24 inch thick pitch pine, and covered her with rolled iron plate. She became a floating fortress powered by an engine driven propeller; she was christened the *Virginia*.

About noon, on March 8, the *Virginia* sailed down the Elizabeth River with her berth deck just awash. She made only five knots, steered badly, and drew 22 feet of water. This untried, experimental vessel with her rolled plates from the Tredegar Foundry in Richmond was a formidable fighting ship. Passing the obstruction on Craney Island, she took to the south channel of Hampton Roads and steered toward Newport News where the frigates, *Congress* and *Cumberland* were lazily swinging by anchor in calm water about a quarter of a mile from shore. The tide was high and the Union sailors were not napping. They sighted her while she was still three quarters of a mile away, "powered up" their 80 guns and fired, but the impact on the *Virginia* was, to the crew, like hail stones falling in a summer's thunderstorm. She came on, never changing course and rammed the *Cumberland*, which sank immediately, taking with her the *Virginia's* iron ram. The *Congress*, trying to avoid a like fate, ran aground and caught fire from exploding shells coming from the *Virginia's* 40 guns. Early in the morning of the next day, the unquenched fire spread to her magazines and she literally burst apart.

Having destroyed these two ships, the *Virginia* turned about and proceeded toward Fortress Monroe accompanied by the *Beaufort* and the

Raleigh. Before the *Virginia* attacked, they had been on the James River. Now, they joined her in an engagement against the Union fleet anchored near the fortress. It consisted of the *Minnesota*, the *Roanoke*, the *Saint Lawrence*, and several smaller gunboats. No one could deny that these naval battles were undisputed victories for the Rebels. At the end of the day, only the *Minnesota* remained active in the Union fleet. However, the *Virginia's* captain, Flag Officer Franklin Buchanan, having 21 seamen wounded, including himself, decided to withdraw and pursue the destruction of the *Minnesota* on the next day. He retired to Sewell's Point where he discovered his ram gone, two guns disabled, one anchor missing, the smoke stack crushed, and several steam pipes shot away.

Repairs were made during the evening; and, early the next morning, the *Virginia* returned to battle under the command of Lieutenant Jones, who replaced the wounded Buchanan. As she approached the *Minnesota*, her crew saw a strange iron craft defending the frigate. It was the *Monitor*. John Ericsson, a Swedish engineer, had designed her and supervised her construction at the Greenpoint shipyard at Brooklyn, New York. Her iron, pancake-like hull, carried a single revolving turret gun, which was supplied by the Watervliet Arsenal, a Federal installation, on the west bank of the Hudson River opposite Troy, New York. She was launched on January 30, 1862, and left New York's harbor on February 27. Although, she was first sighted on Chesapeake Bay, March 8, she could not take up her position in Hampton Roads until the next day. Under the command of John Worden, she arrived in time to save the Union fleet. Upon the *Monitor's* arrival, the *Virginia* immediately attacked her and, for eight hours, they exchanged shell after shell with neither one subduing the other. Exhausted of ammunition and weary of the fight, the *Virginia* retired without being able to get near the Union fleet.

Subsequently, the *Virginia* needed extensive repairs and did not return for combat on Hampton Roads until April 11; but, once she did return, she ruled, uncontested, for 27 days. The Union fleet, including the *Monitor*, had moved into Chesapeake Bay. Defensively, General Wool ordered a 15 inch Rodman Gun, later renamed a Lincoln Gun, mounted on shore near the lighthouse next to two other long range artillery pieces. These guns had the power to destroy the *Virginia*, and they would have done so if she had decided to come through the channel which separated Hampton Roads and the Chesapeake Bay. For almost a month, this naval stalemate persisted.

Our regiment played a minimal role in this crisis. We had been sent to Newport News on the first day of the *Virginia's* attack. Following the destruction of the *Cumberland* and the *Congress*, Wool thought that the Rebels would invade Camp Butler. As a consequence, he sent three regiments from Camp Hamilton, including ours, to reinforce the garrison there. However, the invasion never materialized, and we were withdrawn.

On May 9, following one of her routine patrols of Hampton Roads, the *Virginia* returned to Norfolk for engine repairs and noticed that no flag was flying over the city. The Confederates had evacuated. Their occupation force of 15,000 had withdrawn and proceeded to the defense of Richmond. Consequently, Josiah Tatnall, who had assumed command of the Ironclad in place of Buchanan, realized that he could no longer use the naval base at Portsmouth near Norfolk as a refuge. He tried to lighten the craft so as to navigate on the James River, but the attempt made her unmanageable. He gave the order, "Scuttle the ship!" Obediently, on May 11, the crew blew her up at Craney Island, after which event they proceeded to Drewey's Bluff on the James River south of Richmond. Subsequently, the Federal fleet took command of Hampton Roads and the James River as far north as Harrison's Landing.

With the Federal navy establishing complete superiority around the Peninsula, McClellan felt most confident about his plan to clear the Confederates from the Peninsula and take Richmond. On March 17 he outlined his campaign plans to his generals. He told them that the Army of the Potomac would concentrate at Urbana on the lower Rappahannock River, proceed to West Point at the eastern terminal of the Richmond-York Railroad and, from there, move directly across the Peninsula to Richmond. From supply depots outside of Richmond, it would either put the city under siege or move across the James River and attack Richmond from the rear. McClellan then emphasized, "The *Virginia* has been destroyed. We have a clear supply line up both the York and James Rivers. Fortress Monroe will be our primary base of operations."

To clear the Peninsula of Rebels, McClellan considered his alternatives. He could land his troops north of Gloucester and move to West Point, or he could land below Yorktown, capture it, and cut off the Confederates occupying the region south of it. He had 145,000 men, whom he brought down from Alexandria, and he hoped to procure 10,000 more from Fortress Monroe.

However, when McClellan arrived at Fortress Monroe, on April 2, he was informed, by Stanton, that he could use neither the troops stationed at Camp Hamilton nor those at Camp Butler unless Wool approved. Stanton re-emphasized to him, "You are not in command of Wool's Department." McClellan made the request, but Wool refused to honor it! Hence, on April 4, although irritated, McClellan proceeded toward Yorktown with the troops he had available. On April 22, he was reinforced by General William B. Franklin's division, which joined him at West Point. After a few weeks of hard fighting, the Army of the Potomac broke into the fortifications at Yorktown and Williamsburg and sent the Rebels in retreat toward Richmond. Then McClellan set up a permanent advanced base of operations at White House Landing at the confluence of the York and Pamunkey Rivers.

Once established there, he made a reorganization of the corps and commands of the Army of the Potomac. The new composition follows: Second Corps, General Edwin Sumner; Third Corps, General Samuel Heintzelman; Fourth Corps, General Erasmus Keyes; Fifth Corps, General Fitz-John Porter; and Sixth Corps, General William Franklin. Each had two divisions. In the Sixth Corps, General Henry Slocum was in command of the first division, and the second division was led by General William Smith. In Smith's division were three brigades. The first had troops from Maine, New York, Pennsylvania, and Wisconsin; the second was composed entirely of men from Vermont; the third had one regiment filled with recruits from Maine; and the rest were from New York State. On June 4, our regiment, while still at Fortress Monroe, was informed that it would be assigned to the Sixth Corps. When we eventually came to the front, we joined the third brigade of Smith's second division.

Before we actually joined the Sixth Corps, Smith's division was very active, especially, during the siege of Yorktown and Williamsburg. Subsequent to these campaigns, it moved up the Peninsula; and, by May 30, it was camped on the north side of the Chickahominy River near Mechanicsville. However, it did not participate in the battles of Fair Oaks and Seven Pines on the south side of the river because it could not cross the Chickahominy. Bad weather had set in at that time, and the bridges across the river were washed away. We observed men feverishly repairing them when we arrived at the Chickahominy on June 13. However, before I continue describing other conditions which we found upon arriving at the Chickahominy, let me digress. Prior to June 4, a set of stormy political events took place in and around Fortress Monroe, events which affected our status there and influenced our selection to join the Sixth Corps at the front.

On April 28, 1862, Max Weber was promoted to the rank of brigadier general. This was done at the request and urging of General Wool. For several months, Weber had been seeking a field command, and he thought, "With the Peninsula Campaign becoming a reality, I know that, somehow, I can become part of it." Wool was convinced that Weber would make a good brigade commander and suggested to McClellan that Weber be given a brigade in the Army of the Potomac. However, since Wool had not released troops to McClellan's command on April 4, McClellan opposed Wool's request. Although Weber did not get the command, he did receive the promotion, and Wool created a command for him out of the troops Weber already supervised at Camp Hamilton. In this way, Weber became an equal to Generals Carr and Mansfield, who had their staffs and brigades with them at Fortress Monroe.

When Weber received his promotion, a decision had to be made concerning our leadership. At that time, Ernst Mattais Peter von Vegesack, a Swede with rank of major, was aide-de-camp to General Wool. He was on "leave of absence" from Gustavus Adolphus' Dalarne Regiment.

Adolphus was the King of Sweden and his Dalarne Regiment was held in high esteem by all Swedes. In that Regiment, Vegesack had held the rank of captain and fought the Prussians during their intervention in Schleswig-Holstein in 1848. In 1861, Vegesack came to Washington with the recommendation of Duke August, the King's brother. While Vegesack was at Fortress Monroe, he observed our regiment and became friendly with our officers. He could speak German fluently. He was a knight-errant who longed for glory on the battlefield. Having seen our United Turner Rifles in training, he was convinced that we had the potential to be excellent fighting men, and he desired to be appointed our commander. He placed his request before General Wool who discussed it with Weber. Weber concluded, "Since Vegesack is not a Turner, not even German, I do not believe he should receive the appointment. I suggest that Lieutenant Colonel Francis Weiss be promoted and given my command." So, it was done! Vegesack, disappointed, resigned his commission as major. However, immediately, he re-enlisted, incognito, as a private in Fitz-John Porter's Fifth Corps. Subsequently, in the early stages of the Peninsula Campaign, he distinguished himself in the battles of Yorktown, Williamsburg, and Hanover Court House.

When the battle of Yorktown was concluded and the area secured, McClellan reviewed the troops accompanied by the Prince de Joinville, the Comte de Paris, and the Duc de Chartres. They recognized Vegesack and questioned McClellan, "How can the Union army waste such talent having this man serve as a private?" McClellan, immediately, breveted him to the rank of major and made him an aide-de-camp on his staff. After this promotion, Vegesack performed excellent reconnaissance activity for General Butterfield on May 27 at Hanover Court House. Further, on June 27, at Gaines's Mill, Vegesack heroically aided Fitz-John Porter's troops in their retreat after the Confederates broke the Federal lines.

Following the Seven Days Battle, Vegesack was given command of our regiment while we were in camp at Harrison's Landing. He retained it until we were mustered out in June of 1863, after which he, immediately, took another command and distinguished himself at the Battle of Gettysburg. Following that battle, he learned of the army's denial of his promotion to the rank of brigadier general which he had requested in May, 1863. The army's refusal of his promotion had occurred even though Count Piper of the Swedish Legation in Washington interceded on his behalf. In August, 1863, he resigned and returned to Sweden. Not until the year 1893 were his heoric actions and leadership during the Civil War recognized by our Federal Government. Finally, he was awarded the Congressional Medal of Honor. In order to wear the medal, he was required to receive permission in writing from the King of Sweden. The King responded in the affirmative. However, it's a wonder that the King would give permission in light of the denial of Vegesack's promotion and the failure to recognize his achievements until 30 years had passed. On the contrary, our Turnverein held him in high honor and cordially hosted him in New York when we returned there after our muster-out. My comrades and I were always proud to have served under him.

Unfortunately for us, Francis Weiss was promoted to the rank of colonel and given command of our regiment. He was a good man in civilian life, tall, handsome, meticulous, docile, and prompt. When our regiment was formed, Weber knew of his qualities and chose him as our lieutenant colonel. Furthermore, the leadership of our Turnverein confirmed his appointment. At Fortress Monroe, he assisted seriously with our training but enjoyed more attending social events, at which the ladies commented favorably on his graciousness, manners, dress, and grooming. While on duty, he was most concerned about making mistakes; he looked to his superiors for prior approval of his proposed actions, especially to Colonel Weber. In our daily routine, he would not accept insubordination even in the smallest things. To him, our shoes were never shined enough, and specks of rust were always on our swords and muskets. At each inspection, he would say, "Your buttons need an extra polish; your leather needs another stroke of oil."

After becoming colonel, he added more to his list of fault finding. Passionately, he rebuked our failure to use last names as proper address, our failure to salute, and our failure to enter small details into picket reports. Always, he was most concerned about insignificant infractions concerning the proper care of horses, mules, and wagons. Often he asked, "Have you kept the lane between the horses free from dung?" He grew aloof from his men and non-commissioned officers, but he enjoyed spending much time discussing battle tactics with his equals in other regiments. He liked to exaggerate about his reconnaissance during our Hatteras incident and our attack on Big Bethal.

On arriving at the Chickahominy, he boasted to the other colonels in our brigade that he had brought one of the best trained regiments in the army to join them. He praised our athletic ability and, on one occasion, remarked to Major Thomas W. Hyde, commander of the 7th Maine Regiment, "I brought the Turners here to make the Rebels bleed!" What a contrast between his words and his deeds! During our first experience of cannon fire at Chickahominy, he ordered us to the rear and, falsely, claimed that he was ordered to do so by General Smith. At White Oak Swamp, when General Thomas "Stonewall" Jackson trained his 30 cannons on us, he disappeared, never to be seen again! As a result, our regiment had to make the withdrawal to Malvern Hill without a colonel in command.

After the war, some veterans of the 7th Maine Regiment sarcastically said, "We saw him running a beer garden in Cincinnati." This was their way of emphasizing that he was still running from White Oak Swamp. His lack of leadership under fire cost our regiment a great deal of suffering and humiliation. Also, our Turnverein never included his name in any of their reminiscences and the veterans would admit that they had only two colonels: Weber and Vegesack!

On May 1, after Weiss was promoted to the rank of colonel, General Wool urged the War Department to occupy Norfolk. On May 4, Stanton telegraphed Wool, "What is the condition of the troops?" Wool responded, "The men and ammunition are excellent, but our supply of horses is inadequate." Nonetheless, Chase, Stanton, and Lincoln arrived at Fortress Monroe on May 5. They announced to the newspapers that they wished to visit McClellan, who was in camp at Yorktown; but, actually, they were there to witness the invasion of Norfolk. Wool and Flag Officer Louis Goldsborough synchronized their plans so that while an amphibious assault was being made at Ocean View, Lincoln would be watching from the Rip Raps the bombardment of Sewell's Point. The Rip Raps was the man-made fort in the channel which separated the Peninsula from the vicinity around Norfolk. Before the war, it was called Fort Calhoun; but after Butler was relieved of command at Fortress Monroe, it was renamed Fort Wool. On May 9, at 2 P.M., troops, cannons, and equipment were loaded on canal boats at the dock near the lighthouse. The advanced force was led by newly appointed General Weber and included the 10th, 20th, and 99th New York Regiments, the 16th Massachusetts Regiment, the First New York Mounted Rifles, and three batteries of light artillery.

At dawn on May 10, we disembarked at Ocean View and Colonel Weiss led us along a newly cut road to Tanner's Creek, where we found the bridge burning. Much confusion in command followed, and several regiments were "stumbling over" each other. It was a blessing that the enemy was not present! Finally, General Wool arrived at the head of the column, turned us about, made us retrace our steps to the crossroad, and ordered us to proceed by the old road to the entrenchments before Norfolk. When we reached the entrance to the city at 5 P.M., we were met by the mayor who surrendered with the longest filibuster I have ever heard. While he was being so graciously verbal, the Rebel rear guard was burning the navy yard and destroying all the military equipment which it was unable to carry off.

While this comedy of errors was taking place in front of Norfolk, Lincoln was watching from the parapet at Fortress Monroe. He called General Joseph Carr to his side and said, "Why are your regiments not over in Norfolk?" Carr replied, "I have been asked to wait orders." The president then turned to General Joseph Mansfield and asked the same question. Mansfield responded, "I have been ordered to the fort." Lincoln, in anger, threw his tall hat on the ground and shouted, "Get me someone who can write an order!" Post-haste, Mansfield and Carr went to the battle. When Norfolk and the surrounding area were secured, newspapers lavishly described the battle and presented the story as a great victory for the Union. What ballooning of the truth! In actuality, the Confederates' major force had abandoned the city the day before the invasion.

Our regiment returned to Camp Hamilton. Stanton wrote a commendation for General Wool and his troops on May 11. However, McClellan again demanded sole command of all the forces near him, including Wool's. Lincoln acquiesced and the Department of Southeastern Virginia came under McClellan's authority. As a result, Wool resigned his command and transferred to Fort McHenry, in Maryland. Subsequently, Major General John A. Dix was placed in authority over the artillery units at the fortress and the troops occupying the Norfolk area as far south as Suffolk, Virginia. Later, this force was specified as the Seventh Corps. Weber held a command in this corps until he was assigned to General French's division.

Now, with the Department of Southeastern Virginia under his command, McClellan could move troops of his choice from Camp Hamilton and Camp Butler to the front. We were soon affected. On June 4, Colonel Weiss was ordered to embark our regiment and proceed up the York River to White House Landing, where, upon arrival, we were to go by rail to the Chickahominy River. We arrived at Savage's Station on June 13, which was just one year after leaving New York on the *Alabama*. We were accompanied to the front by the 1st, 2nd, 7th, and 101st New York Regiments, the 16th and 29th Massachusetts Regiments, and the 1st Michigan Regiment. After marching north to a bivouac area which was north of the river facing Mechanicsville, we went into camp with the Third Brigade, Second Division, of the Sixth Corps. We were greeted by its regiments: the 7th Maine Regiment, and the 49th, 77th, and 33rd New York Regiments.

Coming into camp, our regiment was a source of humor for the brigade. Weiss had us outfitted in our dress uniforms and polished shoes as we greeted, for the first time, the mud soaked, rain drenched veterans who had come to the Chickahominy by way of hard fighting up the Peninsula. Also, our conical hats brought smirks and laughter from the veterans as they babbled an imitation of our language and called us "The Germans; The Blackguards!" We did not find this greeting pleasant.

The area in which we made camp was not much more pleasant. The Chickahominy River rises about 15 miles northwest of Richmond and unites with the James River about 40 miles below the city. It, ordinarily, is 40 feet wide, fringed with a dense growth of trees and bordered by low, marshy land, which extends several yards inland from the shoreline. In flash floods, the shoreline disappears. Then, the river's width may extend a full half mile. Even when the rains are moderate, the marsh area is soft and yielding. Strong bridges are needed to make a convenient crossing.

When our brigade arrived on May 24, all the bridges except one, at Mechanicsville, had been destroyed. For a complete month the Army of the Potomac rebuilt them between the Meadows Bridge, north of Mechanicsville, to the Bottom Bridge, below the crossing of the Richmond-York Railroad with the Williamsburg Stage Road. Here, Savage's Station, on the rail line, was set up as an advanced supply depot and field hospital. Opposite the New Bridge, the Mechanicsville Bridge, and the Meadow Bridge, high bluffs overlooked the river and provided excellent positions for Rebel artillery. Then, there was the rain! It rained continuously from the end of May until June 20. Our army's maneuvering was hampered by this continuous rain; and, as soon as the bridges were repaired, they were again swept away or damaged. McClellan may have planned his campaign carefully, but the weather would not cooperate.

Quickly, we had to be brought up to date as to the events which took place there before we arrived. We were informed that, as May ended, McClellan had sent troops from Mechanicsville to Hanover Court House to destroy all rail lines leading north from Richmond to Ashland. He intended to isolate the Rebels by cutting off their supplies and to protect the right flank of his army, which was spread out along the river. We learned also that, at the end of May, General Samuel P. Heintzelman and General Erasmus D. Keyes had been on the south side of the river about four miles from Richmond. The rest of the army was on the north side but could not cross over because the ground was so thoroughly soaked. The Federals and the Confederates clashed at Fair Oaks and Seven Pines. The total burden of the battle had to be carried by the men of Heintzelman's and Keyes's corps. The battles had little military consequence, but the citizens of Richmond saw, for the first time, the horrors of war as their dead and wounded were brought into their city.

After the battles of Fair Oaks and Seven Pines, neither army wanted to engage the other. They wished to wait for the weather to clear. Confederate General Joseph Johnston was severely wounded at Fair Oaks and General Robert E. Lee was given command of all Confederate forces in Virginia. Immediately, Lee realized the seriousness of the Federals' being camped, in force, less than ten miles from Richmond. He considered two choices. He could have his troops remain in the city and prepare for a siege or he could attempt to outmaneuver McClellan, bring him to battle, and, if successful in defeating him, drive the Army of the Potomac from its gates. To initiate his second choice, he would have to divide his forces, a tactically dangerous thing to do. Also, besides waiting for the rain to cease, he would have to wait until Thomas "Stonewall" Jackson could arrive from the Shenandoah Valley. While he waited and pondered his decision, McClellan did likewise. As soon as the rain would cease, he, also, was ready to take the offensive, beginning with an attack on Old Tavern, an attack which would outflank the Rebels behind their redoubts at Mechanicsville. Following up with a frontal attack, he felt, he could throw the Confederates back into Richmond. Then, his siege could begin.

Suddenly, the skies cleared and the entire Army of the Potomac moved to the south side of the river with the exception of Fitz-John Porter's corps. After crossing, the army made a line of defense stretching from Golding's Farm in the north to White Oak Swamp in the south. Franklin's Sixth

Corps, which included us, was at the extreme right in the north, Heintzelman's and Sumner's corps were in the center, and Keyes's corps was at the extreme left in the south. It was June 20, 1862.

For the next five days, we patiently waited for new orders. On June 25, we heard rumors that the Confederates had attacked some Union troops which were advancing along the Williamsburg Road near Oak Grove. However, we were unaware that these skirmishes would later be considered as the beginning of the Seven Days Battle of 1862.

Our position was near the Woodbury Bridge, across which on the north side was Gaines's Mill and Cold Harbor. Opposing the two divisions in our corps, containing fourteen regiments, were the Rebel forces led by General John B. Magruder and General Benjamin Huger. By sundown on June 26, we were ready to carry out our part of McClellan's offensive. Five batteries of artillery were located behind us, spread systematically along the ridge. We were given five days' rations: pork, beans, bread, rice, tea, sugar, vinegar, and several quarts of molasses. That night, we went to sleep, fearful; but we were confident that, on the morrow, we would have a great victory. We were unaware that Lee would go on the offensive first. That night he did so!

At 8:30 A.M., on June 27, Franklin received orders from McClellan not to make our planned attack. He was told to go on the defensive, keep Smith's division in place, and send Slocum's division to support Porter. McClellan informed Franklin that Lee had turned the Union flank north of the river and was attacking in our rear with the bulk of his army! Slocum moved at once; but, upon reaching the Woodbury Bridge, he was recalled. It was impossible to understand why this recall order was given.

At 10:30 A.M., Magruder and Huger opened fire on our lines with five or ten batteries. Shells began bursting everywhere, but we could not see the enemy. Whom and how were we supposed to fight? Suddenly, I saw shells fall in the middle of the 49th New York Regiment, and several bodies were thrown into the air. Immediately after, shells burst within our ranks. Colonel Weiss gave an order, "Run for the trees!" We broke ranks and ran to the woods, almost breaking the ranks of the 7th Maine Regiment as we darted forth. Major Hyde shouted, "The Germans are breaking like glass! Get them back in ranks!" We paid him no attention but continued to follow Weiss.

At 11:30 A.M., the shelling stopped, and we returned to our positions on the line. When questioned as to why we broke and ran, Colonel Weiss said, "General Smith told me to have the men withdraw and accept a charge at the edge of the woods." Later, it was discovered that this order was never given. However, wouldn't we have broken like glass even if we had been ordered to stand our ground? It is quite possible that "green troops" under cannon fire for the first time with no enemy in sight to fight would have chosen to run! Years later, after the war, I questioned the rationale of committing suicide when prudence encouraged an alternative action; but, in war, the soldier learns to obey and stay. Only strong leadership pushes one to stand and die! We did not have such leadership in Colonel Weiss!

In the afternoon, Slocum was again called upon to help Porter. He moved quickly. As soon as his division arrived at Gaines's Mill, it was engaged. Now, almost all of Lee's army was on the north side of the river, but we were unaware of this, nor were we aware of the seriousness of the Federal situation. The heavy enfilading on our side, by Magruder and Huger, made us believe that the main attack was directed against us. Also, the dense woods along the river prevented us from hearing the intense cannonading taking place only two miles away at Gaines's Mill and Cold Harbor.

At five o'clock, after repeatedly warding off the violent and continuous onslaught of the Rebels, Porter's line broke, and the enemy poured through. At the same time, we were fiercely attacked on our extreme right. An intense skirmish resulted. The enemy was turned back; but, as the sun was setting, the opposing forces were in some places only 50 yards apart. However, this attack served its purpose. Again, it held us from changing our position and going to the aid of Porter.

Although Porter's command was in rout, and the field at Gaines's Mill was lost to the Confederates, all the troops on our side of the river were intact. Subsequently, Porter retreated across the Woodbury Bridge, and Slocum returned to our lines. His division was badly mauled! Now, the enemy was behind us, in front of us, and to the right of us. Quickly, the engineers demolished all the bridges so as to keep the main body of Lee's army on the north side of the river. However, the Army of the Potomac was cut off from its base of supply.

In late evening, at the Trent House, McClellan's headquarters, a strategy meeting of the corps commanders was held. They decided that an orderly withdrawal should be carried out. McClellan, disliking the word retreat, called it a change in base. It was decided that the Army of the Potomac would move all — men, artillery, animals, and equipment south to Harrison's Landing some 29 miles away. There, it would regroup and plan another attack on Richmond. Our division was chosen to be the rear guard for this retreat; and, with the tide of battle having shifted to the enemy's advantage, we knew that it had a difficult task. Nonetheless, we were determined to do what was necessary to allow the Army of the Potomac to walk out intact!

On the morning of June 28, we moved across the cornfield to the rear of Golding's Farm and established another defensive position. With the bridges destroyed, Confederate forces on the north side of the river were neutralized for a time. Hence, we felt that we could effectively cover the army's movement south through the fields and hills, which were surrounded by a swamp shaped like a fish hook. The "door" through the hook was the White Oak Bridge eight miles due south of Golding's Farm. The entire Army of the Potomac would have to go through that door! About halfway between our position and the bridge was Savage's Station. First, we had to delay the Rebels until the main body of our army reached it.

While performing our delaying action, we were attacked by two Georgia regiments, but they were repulsed. Gradually, we pulled back. The 49th Pennsylvania Regiment and the 33rd New York Regiment were the last to give up their positions. At nightfall, we slept on our weapons about a mile north of Savage's Station. Jackson's division north of the river was busily repairing bridges. Soon, its task would be completed, and Jackson's entire army would come down upon us. No matter what his strength might be, we planned to stop him at Savage's Station on the following day.

Sunday, June 29, was clear and sunny. We took up our positions at the station; and, about 2 P.M., we were violently attacked. Our lines held while the Army of the Potomac passed through them in an orderly fashion but with haste. General John Sedgwick's troops of Sumner's corps were the last to come through. We closed ranks behind them and took up a new line of defense. Smith spread out our three brigades in the woods southwest of the station. In the clearing to our north, some 2,500 wounded were being attended to at a field hospital behind which was the Trent House. In the distance, we saw boxes, filled with hard bread, burning. Barrels of whiskey and huge amounts of medical supplies were also being destroyed. Obviously, the Federals were trying to destroy everything so it would not fall into Rebel hands. Suddenly, a tremendous explosion took place; stores of ammunition and powder were ignited. What a holocaust! Flames and smoke filled the sky!

As we waited for the Rebel attack, we had very little water. We chewed on twigs to assuage our thirst. At five o'clock, the attack came. Our center was being held by the Second Brigade of our division, which was led by General William T. Brooks. It moved forward. His Vermonters counterattacked and fought until darkness. They suffered heavy losses, but the enemy was held off. During their engagement, Colonel Weiss was ordered to take our regiment forward and reinforce Brooks's troops. Weiss delayed in making the advance, and we did not reach Brooks until the battle was over. At the end of the day, most of the army was safely across the White Oak Bridge and out of immediate danger. Subsequently, it moved south to Long Bridge Road, turned east to Glendale, and again turned south to Malvern Hill, where McClellan was forming a formidable line of defense by employing a massive concentration of artillery.

As darkness came, Jackson cut off his pursuit of the Army of the Potomac. This was opportune for us. We were able to slip away and head for the White Oak Bridge. We crossed the bridge at 3 A.M. on Monday, June 30. On the south side of the bridge, we saw that the road rose quickly. We ascended and settled in a clearing at the crest about 200 yards from the bridge. We turned and faced the swamp which we had just crossed. General William Brooks's and General Winfield Hancock's brigades were stationed about 200 yards to the right and rear of us. On our left was an extension of the swamp, running parallel to the road and perpendicular to the swamp. It was a deep ravine about a mile and a half long, terminating near Long Bridge Road. It was overgrown with trees and brush on the edges and filled with muddy water, stumps, and broken branches.

On the other side of this ravine was a clearing like the one in which we were bivouacked. In order to reach it, the engineers built a bridge over the ravine near the edge of the swamp. General Henry Naglee's brigade of Keyes's corps and General Thomas Meagher's brigade of Sumner's corps bivouacked in the clearing close to the edge of the swamp. This placed them left and front of us, but the trees that lined the ravine hid them from our view. Other units of Sumner's corps held a line behind Naglee and Meagher. These units were parallel with Naglee and Meagher but still forward from us.

Smith made his headquarters in a farm house on our right in front of Hancock and Brooks. The First and Third New York Volunteer Artillery, along with the 5th U.S. Artillery, which was under the command of Colonel Romeyn Ayres, was set up in front of Smith's headquarters.

The last of Sumner's corps, General Israel Richardson's division, came across the White Oak Bridge just before 10 A.M. It was assigned the task of blowing the bridge. The men set the charges and were ready to ignite them when, at a high gallop, Captain George Hazard with his entire artillery unit came across. It was being chased by Jackson's advanced guard. When it was safely on our side of the swamp, the charges went off. Jackson's troops were stranded on the other side. Following this event, Richardson crossed the ravine and set his men down in the clearing behind Sumner's other division, which was already in place. When Richardson's troops were finally settled, they were on a line with Brooks and Hancock, who were on our side of the ravine. Hazard set up his artillery in front of Richardson on a line with Ayres. Together, Hazard and Ayres could bring an excellent cross fire onto the bridge if Jackson decided to repair and cross it. General John Caldwell's brigade, in Richardson's division, was closest to us but across the ravine. In his brigade, the 5th New Hampshire Regiment and the 7th New York Regiment were stationed at the ravine's edge. The 7th New York Regiment, a German regiment, now under the command of Colonel George Shack, included many of our friends from New York City.

By 10:30 A.M., Jackson's entire force was on the north side of the swamp and, finding the bridge destroyed, began to mount artillery on a high ridge overlooking our positions. Later, this high ground was called Cedar Ridge. It is questionable how many cannons were placed there, but there were at least 30.

From 10:30 A.M. until noon, our side of the swamp was very peaceful. It was so peaceful that General Smith decided to take a bath. At high noon, just as he was relaxed in the tub, Jackson opened fire with all his cannons simultaneously and without warning. The earth shook! Shell after shell came down on us like rain; trees were uprooted, wagons smashed, tents destroyed; groups of men died on the spot where they sipped their last cup of coffee! Mule teams, watering at the edge of the swamp, ran helter-skelter trampling surprised, relaxed, and unprepared soldiers. Finding cover was the only thought in everyone's mind. Smith's bath was abruptly ended as a shell exploded inside the farmhouse. He was unharmed; but, the owner, who stayed to protect his chickens from being ravaged by the Yankees, had his leg shattered, and he bled to death! Captain Hazard was, instantly, killed as a shell demolished one of his batteries.

Our brigade was ordered to withdraw down the road. All of our regiments moved except us. We were in the foremost advanced position and did not hear the order. Momentarily, the cannons ceased firing and, finding ourselves alone, we shouted, "Sergeant, what are our orders?" He replied, "I have none; I cannot find Colonel Weiss!" A voice came from the far right side of the line, "Weiss wants you over with Hancock's brigade." This was followed by a contradictory notice, "Weiss is gone! Find Colonel Shack; he will know what to do!" We rose from our prone positions. At that instant, and again without warning, Jackson's cannons poured shells directly at us. One shell burst in the middle of our line and the men split. Half of them ran toward Hancock and the other half went toward Shack, plunging into the ravine as they did so. I was with the latter group.

Those who went into the ravine were engulfed waste deep in the mud. Some lost their muskets as they tore loose; others were lacerated by broken branches or sprained their ankles. Those who tore loose ran toward General Caldwell's brigade. When he saw them coming toward him without muskets, he was furious. He gave an order to his 5th New Hampshire Regiment, "Boys, stand firm! Raise your bayonets! Run those skulkers through!" Our men kept coming, shouting in German that they were joining Colonel Shack. The New Englanders, not understanding German, stood as ordered, and bayoneted the first group which met their line. Shack, hearing the Germans' cry, gave a quick translation to General Caldwell, who immediately rescinded the order. The General was mortified!

On the right side of the road, the open field was dotted with our conical hats and knapsacks. The group of Turners going toward Hancock took only their muskets and whatever clothes they were wearing at the time the blast split our regiment. Major Hyde, who was about a half mile down the road with his 7th Maine Regiment, claims that he saw the Turners running away with Colonel Weiss leading the flight. Later, he suggested a poem that could describe the event;

I'll shplit dem like Kartoffels;
I'll slog 'em on de Kop;
I'll set the blackguards roonin
So they don't know ven to stop!

Neither I nor anyone else in my company ever recalls seeing Colonel Weiss again. Only in hushed tones was he spoken of by the men of our regiment. I can still hear them say, "Weiss war ein Drueckeberger. Er wurde abgesetzt, weil er in der blutigen Schlacht auf Halbinsel durch Abwesenheit glaenzte." Their sarcasm was justified. Weiss was truly a shirker of duty, and he did "distinguish" himself in the bloody battle at White Oak Swamp on the Peninsula by his absence.

I stayed in the ravine, helping my comrades who were injured. Sporadically, the shelling continued all afternoon. Later, we moved down the ravine away from the noise. When it was dark, we emerged near Long Bridge Road. Upon reaching the road, we found other stragglers, who informed us that our regiment had withdrawn and moved south to Glendale. A wounded soldier, from the 33rd New York Regiment, told us that the Turners had been regrouped by Captain Martindale of General Davidson's staff, and Lieutenant Colonel Engelbert Schnepf was placed in command. By late afternoon, Jackson had found a way to ford the swamp and was in pursuit of the Union rear guard. However, he was too late to trap the Army of the Potomac at Glendale and would not engage it again until he reached Malvern Hill. Unfortunately, he was not too late to make us his prisoners!

I can only describe the battle at Malvern Hill, which was fought on July 1, 1862, from secondhand information. Fifty other Turners and I, who were captured as we emerged from the ravine, were taken to prison on Belle Isle, which was a rocky, desolate island in the middle of the James River next to Richmond. However, I understand that the Federal forces held a high ground at Malvern Hill, where they massed a huge number of batteries. From this defensive position, they waited for the Confederates to attack them. Before them lay a large open field, the edge of which was densely wooded. Suddenly, from these woods, the Rebels emerged and, without concern or fear, charged up the hill. The Federals cut them down unmercifully. For the first time in the war, the Federals unleashed upon the enemy enormous shells weighing 268 pounds. One Rebel officer remarked, "I don't know why we are making this charge. This is not war; this is murder!" Later, another Confederate general said, "After seeing what I have seen today, if the Union artillery were on the same field with the Confederate infantry, no power on earth could match them!" When the smoke had cleared from the battlefield, the Federal artillery and some infantry stayed in defensive positions; the Rebels returned to Richmond. The Seven Days Battle of 1862 had come to an end. Subsequently, the Army of the Potomac dug in at Harrison's Landing.

In the final stage of the retreat to Harrison's Landing, the 20th New York Regiment battled the Rebels at Turkey Creek. The regiment defended two bridges across the creek until the army was safely on the south side. Then Lieutenant Colonel Schneph ordered the Turners to destroy the bridges. Subsequently, the Turners withdrew in an orderly manner.

During the month of July, I lingered as a prisoner. With me were 7,000 Federals, who had been taken prisoners during the Seven Days Battle. From our brigade, besides those of our regiment, five men of the 7th Maine Regiment, 19 from the 33rd New York Regiment, and 11 from the 77th New York Regiment were also imprisoned. Conditions on Belle Isle were disgusting! Thankfully, on August 6, several hundred others and I were exchanged at Aiken's Landing, which was located north of Jones Neck on the James River. We were sent down river by steamer to Harrison's Landing where I rejoined my regiment on August 16.

While in prison, I met some members of the 16th New York Regiment from Slocum's division. They had been wounded at Gaines's Mill and sent to the field hospital at Savage's Station. In our retreat, it was impossible to evacuate them, and they were also made prisoners. Before the Seven Days Battle, Mrs. Howland, their colonel's wife, had presented their entire regiment with white straw hats with wide brims. They wore these in the battle and were so conspicuous that the Rebels deliberately trained their cannons on them. After this tragedy, one would think that the other members of their regiment would have discarded these hats, but they continued to wear them all through the retreat to Harrison's Landing. I believe our Turners had a similar problem. At the defense of White Oak Bridge, when we began to evacuate, Jackson must have been attracted to our conical hats with the green pom-pons and fired his cannons directly at us. However, after our experience, we discarded those hats as part of our combat uniform.

The news of our alleged cowardice reached the Verein in New York. The members were horrified! We had disgraced them! How could they ever forgive us? Many times since, I have reflected on this question and I believe that they over-reacted. Their vision was myopic, filled with emotion but not realistic. They were victims of a Civil War mentality, the "heroic" mentality. Did they understand that we were human, not stone idols? Before these seven days of battle, we had never been asked to restrain our nerves under heavy fire. We had not learned how to act as a unit in the event of losing our leadership. Quick changes of command under combat conditions had never been practiced. Really, could such changes ever have been practiced? Furthermore, during those seven days, we were for the first time becoming the battle scarred soldiers which we had not been before. For the first time, we saw our comrades mangled! For the first time, we experienced wholesale death! We had not yet learned contempt for that kind of death, but familiarity with it begets contempt for it. For the first time, we learned that becoming detached from the whole unit was stupidity. It put 51 of us in prison where life was a most painful ordeal. Our experience in those seven days and the month that followed hardened us, and we vowed that, because of our consequent self discipline, the nation, our friends, and our enemies would not see us split up again. However, being human, we could not predict the future and guarantee that our vow would be inviolable. Furthermore, our strongest feeling was one of betrayal by our leadership. We deserved better! Thank God, we eventually got it!

When I rejoined my regiment, it was camped just outside the stone enclosure of Westover Church south of Herring Creek about a mile and a half from the James River. Trenches had been dug and redoubts constructed, surrounding the two plantations at Berkley and Westover. We had excellent protection from an attack by land, and we were well supplied and protected by the steamers and gunboats in the river. The entire complex in which we bivouacked was called Harrison's Landing. The Army of the Potomac's 140,000 soldiers occupied it for over a month. This many crowded in one place can do a huge amount of damage in a short time. At Berkley, all the trees in a mile wide strip of land from the mansion to the river were cut down in 48 hours after the arrival of the army. The beautiful and expensive furniture in the mansion was broken up for firewood. Ornate tables were converted for surgery and soaked with human blood. Once, McClellan in a fit of rage, cut down the parlor chandelier with one swipe of his sword.

However, my stay at Harrison's Landing left me with one very pleasant memory. One evening, after returning from Belle Isle, I heard, for the first time, the bugler render a very chilling tune. He played the melancholy sound of taps as dusk settled over the James River. While I had been a prisoner, the tune had been composed at Berkley by General Daniel Butterfield. It was first played in the evening of the day on which it was composed. Each evening after that day, while it was played on our side of the James River, the tune was taken up by the Confederates across the river and played back like a haunting echo.

Lincoln came twice to visit the army and had long discussions with McClellan. The president tried to understand the reasons for the Army of the Potomac's failure to take Richmond. McClellan, the young Napoleon, became antagonistic toward the president and was relieved of his command. Later, he was reinstated after General John Pope was defeated at the second battle at Bull Run. Many other officers were reprimanded or dismissed. General John Davidson, our brigade commander, was sent to Missouri. He had been held responsible for our conduct at White Oak Bridge. On June 29, he was inflicted with sunstroke prior to the battle at Savage's Station. Colonel Robert F. Taylor of the 33rd New York Regiment was given command of our brigade but General Davidson returned to the command an hour before General Jackson began his artillery barrage on June 30. George Koenig, our first lieutenant, was discharged and Francis Weiss was, officially, considered "resigned." Furthermore, from our regiment, 135 enlisted men were dismissed from the service. Vegesack was promoted to the rank of colonel, on July 19, and given command of our regiment. Vegesack was also placed in command of our Third Brigade. He replaced Davidson and held the brigade command, along with our regimental command, until we began the Maryland Campaign. In that campaign Vegesack, although retaining command of our regiment, was replaced as brigade commander by Colonel William Irwin. During the Seven Days Battle, Irwin led the 49th Pennsylvania Regiment, which was attached to the 1st Brigade of our division. It was this brigade, under the command of General Winfield Hancock, that the Turners tried to join when they split at White Oak Bridge on June 30. Furthermore, General Darius Couch's division was added to the Sixth Corps, and General Franklin and General Smith retained their respective commands.

After the war, General Franklin wrote concerning the conduct of the men in our rear guard. He said, "They had been soldiers less than a year, yet their conduct could not have been more soldierly had they seen ten years of service. No such material for soldiers was ever in the field before, and their behavior in this moment foreshadowed their success as veterans at Appomattox." No one has ever said that our regiment was not included in his congratulatory note. Apparently, our conduct at White Oak Swamp must not have been as detrimental as our Turnverein's emotion led us to believe.

Three days after I rejoined my regiment, it was ordered to withdraw from Harrison's Landing. In that withdrawal, we crossed over the Chickahominy River near its entry into the James River. We marched across the longest pontoon bridge constructed during the war. It was built by Company F of the 15th New York Regiment.

By August 21, the Army of the Potomac was back within the protection of Fortress Monroe. Lincoln would not allow any further attempts to attack Richmond by way of the Peninsula. Lee and Jackson had moved north, and Washington was again threatened. The Union and Confederate forces were about to clash again at Bull Run. We were called upon to help.

On August 22, we boarded transports and sailed up the Potomac River. We were scheduled to land at Aquia Creek, but, because the wharves were loaded with too much equipment, we had to find another location to disembark. Finally, on August 25, we landed at Alexandria. We bivouacked at Camp California. On August 28, we were ordered to form columns and move up the Fairfax and Alexandria Pike to Centreville. When we were ready to march, the order was cancelled. There were no horses to pull the wagons and cannons! Our delay in moving was lengthy since our officers had to do a great deal of hassling to obtain them from the capital.

On August 29, we arrived in Annandale, Virginia, with the front only ten miles away, but we were halted again! Smith noticed that each of us had only ten rounds of ammunition. Usually, going into battle, we carried 60 rounds, and he refused to allow us to engage the enemy until the number was increased. Again, there was hassling with the quartermaster corps; but, when the problem was corrected, we proceeded. Unfortunately, by the time we did arrive at Centreville, the second battle at Bull Run had already been fought and lost. The demoralized Union army was again retreating to Washington. We stayed in camp at Centreville until September 1. Subsequently, General Franklin was reprimanded for not getting us to Bull Run in time to help the Union army in the battle.

In the evening of September 1, we marched through Fairfax and returned to Camp California. We remained there until September 6. During our stay, all leaves of absence were cancelled, but some of the officers in the other regiments of our brigade went into the city of Washington to enjoy a bit of frolic at Willard's. However, upon returning, they were reprimanded by Vegesack. We amused ourselves in camp with cards, marbles, and dominoes. During the day, our officers vigorously kept drilling us and by the end of our short stay each of us could load and fire three rounds each minute.

Also, we had to learn the technique of setting up and sleeping under our newly issued shelter tents, which we called dog tents. The army had decided to discard the use of the Sibley tent, a cumbersome conical structure, which slept 18 men lying in a circle with their feet toward the center. With the use of the dog tent, the army encouraged the buddy system. On the march, we carried it in two parts, each man of the buddy team having the matching part of the other. When set up, the tent was six feet long. It was made of two pieces of muslin with borders and had button holes in one piece with matching buttons in the other. It slept two in good weather; but, by adding an extra piece on rainy nights, we could add a third sleeper and still keep our knapsacks dry underneath.

During the night, on September 6, we crossed the Long Bridge over the Potomac and set up camp at Offut's Crossroads. Colonel William H. Irwin replaced Vegesack as brigade commander, and we were told that Lee had invaded Maryland. We marched! On September 8, we marched through Tenallytown and pitched our tents in the evening at Rockville, Maryland. On September 9, we had reached Darnestown and continued on through Dawsonville and Barnesville, reaching Buckeystown on September 12. On the march, at bivouac, we ate chickens, vegetables, honey, apple butter, and pies: the local farmer's daughters brought these to us and gave them graciously. It was quite a contrast to our experience on the Peninsula. There, we ate fat pork and odious beef, which was served, quivering, from an animal heated by a long day's march and killed as soon as the march ended. On the Peninsula, forage was hard to come by; but, in Maryland, wood and water were easy to find, and we had no difficulty finding forage for the horses.

On entering Maryland, we were not sure if the local people were truly loyal to the Union. I knew how the Baltimorians had treated our Turners in April, 1861. Although at first I was suspicious about the political feelings of these Maryland country folks, it did my spirits good to see the Stars and Stripes in other places than above the heads of our color guards. However, I soon came to like these northwestern Marylanders. A particular treat was communicating with them in our native language; it seemed that the population was predominately German. Speaking in German, they told us of their backgrounds and the places they had come from in Europe. One farmer told us that many of them had brought special herbs with them when they immigrated. On the march, I saw the fields covered with pouliolroyal, which the Americans called pennyroyal. It is a perennial mint with small, pungently aromatic, leaves. When you squeeze them, they give forth an oil, which, when rubbed on the skin, keeps the mosquitoes away. However, it was sad to see so many of the plants bruised by the trampling of our thousands of feet.

When we marched through Tenallytown, the sound of our voices could be heard everywhere. We laughed and joked with everyone. By the time we reached Buckeystown, the weight of our knapsacks and muskets had become heavy, and our laughter had long before died out; one heard only the shuffling of our feet, the rubbing and straining of our leather straps, and the flopping of our canteens. Not much emotion was shown in the regiment when Vegesack gave the order, "Spread out in the fields, stack your arms, build fires, and boil your coffee." It was just another order, and we were exhausted!

We camped at Buckeystown until September 14 while the rest of the army, under McClellan, was in Frederick. Couch's division was employed to protect the army's left flank; it was camped at Licksville. Frederick was ten miles northwest of us. There, McClellan had four corps with him. They were: the First Corps under General Joseph Hooker, the Second Corps led by General Edwin Sumner, the Ninth Corps commanded by General Jesse Reno, and the Twelfth Corps under General Joseph Mansfield.

The Confederates, who had occupied Frederick before the Federals arrived, were now on the west side of South Mountain. They were known as General Lee's Army of Northern Virginia. This group consisted of 20 brigades under General James Longstreet, 14 brigades under General Thomas "Stonewall" Jackson, and five brigades under the command of General Daniel H. Hill. The army had with it a considerable amount of cavalry and artillery. It had had a very successful year in 1862. It had cleared the Peninsula of the Army of the Potomac and fought in northeastern Virginia, freeing it of Federals up to the works around Washington. Also, it forced the Union troops occupying Winchester to pull back to Harper's Ferry and Martinsburg. Having achieved all this, Lee decided that it was time to carry the war past the frontier of his commonwealth; and, although he had vowed to lift his hand only against an enemy that would invade his state, he felt that it was now time to carry the war further because the Yankees would not cease invading that state even though he had demonstrated his superiority in battle.

When McClellan reached Frederick he learned that the Rebels had been there and left. A private in an Indiana regiment, while cleaning up one of the camps vacated by them, found General Lee's battle plans wrapped tightly around several cigars. Upon receiving these plans, McClellan was determined to go on the offensive. He decided that, while the main body of his army would pursue Lee through Turner's Gap, our Sixth Corps would cross South Mountain at Crampton's Gap, relieve the Federal forces at Harper's Ferry, and cut off Lee's retreat back into Virginia. We were told to ready ourselves for this campaign on the night of September 13. We moved out of camp the next morning.

At noon, on September 14, we entered Burkittsville and found the Rebels guarding the foot of the pass with artillery and sharpshooters. As we came into the town, cannon balls were crashing into the streets and houses but, nonetheless, the civilians came out to cheer us. Immediately, Slocum placed his division in front of the Rebels. When all were in their assigned positions, he ordered them to charge up the pass under cover of his artillery. Three thousand Union troops engaged two thousand of the enemy and the pass was opened in an afternoon of fighting. Our division was held in reserve. We had no combat that day, but we did help in rounding up 400 prisoners.

That night, we made camp at the summit and set out our pickets. The Rebels retreated down the west side of the mountain. Before dawn, we broke camp and marched in pursuit of them. At the western base of the mountain, we spread out our two divisions in Pleasant Valley near Rohrersville. Unfortunately, the Federals at Harper's Ferry, had already been under Confederate attack and had surrendered to Jackson at dawn on September 15. Nonetheless, Franklin considered offensive action against those Confederates who were still in defensive positions on Maryland Heights above the town of Harper's Ferry. They were directly in front of us. However, Franklin found that Slocum's men were too exhausted to make battle, having sustained the whole burden of the previous day's fighting, and he was convinced that the Rebels outnumbered Smith's division. Hence, we did not attack but went on the defensive and waited new orders from McClellan.

On September 14, McClellan's four corps, which had bivouacked at Frederick while we were in Buckeystown, battled with the Confederates at Turner's Gap on South Mountain. There, at the end of the day, the Rebels had not been dislodged from their defensive positions at the summit of the mountain. However, General Lee knew that he could not contain, for another day, the Union forces which now had their full strength concentrated against him. He retreated from his positions at Turner's Gap, but his army was not demoralized. McClellan called the action on South

Mountain a victory! Lee called it a delaying action! On September 15, Lee, whose forces now seemed to be in retreat, decided to turn and give battle to McClellan in a place of Lee's choice between Antietam Creek and the Potomac River, which was in an area surrounding Sharpsburg. Quickly, both armies put their troops in position and waited. At dawn, on the morning of September 17, the waiting ended. The Union's First Corps, under the command of Hooker, opened the day's fighting. When that day, September 17, 1862, came to an end, the battlefield was so littered with dead and wounded that it has been remembered as the bloodiest day in American history.

Lee's army had been on the march or fighting since June 25; victorious in all campaigns until now. The Federal army had not won a major battle for 85 days before its engagement with the Rebels on South Mountain; the Federals felt the tide had turned. Morale was high on both sides. The Army of Northern Virginia and The Army of the Potomac were now determined to end this war, face to face, in one day! Fortunately, it would be our regiment's fate to be part of that day's fight. Our Turner Rifles had a score to settle. Now the Rebels would compete with a regiment quite different from the one they had seen at the Chickahominy River and at White Oak Swamp. This was war, not a Turnfest, but at no Turnfest in the future would the competition and the prize ever be greater than on the Antietam battlefield. Unfortunately, the price we would pay would be high. The ranks of our Turner Rifles would be filled with dead and wounded!

On September 15 and 16, we bivouacked at Pleasant Valley while the Confederates, who had captured the Union forces and supplies at Harper's Ferry, moved to Antietam. We received no orders to move until 3 A.M. on September 17. Again, we did not move immediately. Only after we had coffee and breakfast did we break camp and begin our march at 5:30 A.M. Obediently, we moved, but we were not told where we were going as we came out of the fields onto the Sharpsburg Road and headed northwest. Soon, we surmised that our destination was Antietam Creek about 12 miles away. We were moving in double-quick step. Irwin had our brigade leading the entire Sixth Corps, and Vegesack had us at the head of our brigade column. Immediately behind us were the 7th Maine Regiment and the 77th New York Regiment. They were followed by the 33rd and the 49th New York Regiments.

At about 9:30 A.M., we heard cannon fire. Suddenly, it grew louder, and we could hear the crack of muskets. We turned off the Sharpsburg Road and headed for the Pry House where McClellan had his headquarters. Hundreds of wounded were being brought to the rear. At a ford just below the Pry House, we crossed the Antietam Creek and proceeded toward the East Woods where the 10th Maine Regiment, which had been reduced to a squad, was prostrate on the ground at the edge of the woods. We stepped lively! As we approached the clearing, we were startled to see "den

Kriegschauplatz!" It was a panorama of the field of battle, which lay before us; the carnage of the fighting, which had raged since early morning, was everywhere: bodies of men, dead and wounded; wagons and barns burned; artillery pieces smashed; men running in confusion; and cornfields soaked in blood.

Someone requested the hour. It was 10 A.M. We came down the Smoketown Road and veered off. Mumma's farmhouse and barns were burning and a huge explosion of a caisson off in the distance hurled clouds of debris into the air. The Confederates' 27th North Carolina Regiment and the 3rd Arkansas Regiment had made a fierce counterattack on General George Greene's Union troops who, earlier, had gained a foothold around Dunker Church. These Rebel regiments drove them back to Mumma's farm. Colonel John Cooke, their leader, had rallied his 675 Confederates, surprised Greene, and routed him. When we first saw them, these opposing forces were in a hand-to-hand struggle near the fence line between the Mumma and Roulette farms. Greene's troops were weakening, but the Rebels were beginning to run out of ammunition.

As our column approached the action, General Smith shouted to Colonel Irwin, "Put that German regiment to the front!" Irwin bellowed to Vegesack, "Have them fix their bayonets and support the troops at the fence." Forward we went; the contact was intense and the Rebels began to break off. Seeing the Rebels weakening, Lieutenant Colonel Schnepf ordered, "Now, push them back! Make them retreat! Pursue them!" Even louder, we heard Irwin repeat many times, "Attack! Attack! Fire low, 20th; fire low!"

We followed Schnepf's orders. In our pursuit, we marched across a plowed field and moved into a cornfield. We turned obliquely to our left and had the Rebels in front of us. The 77th New York Regiment went straight ahead. The 7th Maine Regiment paused to flush out some Rebels who had taken cover in nearby barns. We kept moving; and, when we reached a point midway between Mumma's farm and the Dunker Church, we saw some Federal troops prone on the ground firing at the Confederates. We didn't know to what regiment these Federals were attached, but their enfilading brought down many of the enemy who were surprised by their presence in that part of the field. The Rebels did not expect to be hit from the rear.

As we continued our advance, we passed over about four hundred Confederate bodies lying in death, so neatly you would think that they had originally been a line of upright dominoes, which now lay collapsed one upon the other. We did not pause. Soon, we came upon the Dunker Church and saw before us an abandoned caisson with dead horses and soldiers lying beside it. Again, we did not stop; our charge continued! Suddenly, the Rebels rallied! Grape, shells, and minie-balls came from behind the trees in the West Woods. They fell on us like hail. Men fell! In the line in front of me, I saw Jacob Leier's arm ripped from his body. The line crumbled!

Behind us, Vegesack was erect in his saddle. His pistol flashed in the sun! At that moment, he was the most prominent figure on the battlefield. The charge was glorious! Although we were stopped short of the West Woods, we rallied and lay down on the ridge in front of Dunker Church. We kept up an incessant fire against the woods, and the Rebels' sharpshooters returned the fire. Our colors were raised so high, it seemed as if we were offering the Rebels a perfect target. Major Hyde, whose regiment had taken up a position next to us under cover of rocks, called out, "Vegesack, have your men lower their colors!" Vegesack replied, "No! This is our hour of glory; the men of the 20th have become the soldiers they were trained to be!" For three hours, our banner, Bahn Frei, waved high while the fighting continued. We had taken the line which we were ordered to take, and we held it. It had been lost three times that day, but it would not be lost again! This was the last Federal attack thrown against the Confederate center on that bloodiest day.

I was not fortunate enough to come forth from the charge unscathed. Almost immediately after we rallied on the ridge, I felt a sharp blow against my face. A 58 caliber minie-ball pierced me above the left lower jaw, traveled across the top of my tongue, and lodged in my right cheek below the ear. My musket flew into the air. I fell to the ground unconscious. Later, I found that my comrades had dragged me to a place out of the line of fire.

Regaining consciousness, I went back to Mumma's farm, where I found a spring and bathed my wound. The water was very salty! Our assistant surgeons, George Steinert and Charles Heiland, ordered me and the other wounded from the 20th New York Regiment to be taken to a field hospital which assistant surgeon Richard Curran of the 33rd New York Regiment had set up in the East Woods. Our surgeon, Doctor Hauser, cut the ball from my face and dressed the wound. Othelia Gehrt, from the Verein in New York, acted as nurse. She had taken it upon herself to follow our regiment through many of our battles and assist the doctor. While attending to their duties at Antietam, Doctor Hauser and she were dissatisfied with the care that assistant surgeon Heiland had given to the wounded. Heiland was dismissed from the service on October 4.

The battle ended with sunset and did not resume the next day. Lee surrendered the field to the Federals and slipped away across the Potomac River into Virginia. The main body of our regiment bivouacked at Hagerstown, but I was kept at the field hospital set up on the Hoffman Farm near Smoketown. By October 4, many of our wounded had been transferred to Baltimore. I was one of these. There, I lingered in the hospital until February 17, 1863. Leier remained there another month. We survived but Johann Dienst, a native of Forchheim, my village in Baden, died of the wounds he had received in our charge on Dunker Church. According to the offical records, the 20th New York Regiment had sustained 145 casualties at Antietam. Five officers and 33 enlisted men were killed. Four officers and 92 enlisted men were wounded, and 11 enlisted men were missing. On September 17, the total number of casualties of the Third Brigade, was 342.

After the Battle of Antietam, the 20th New York Regiment remained as part of the Third Brigade, Second Division of the Sixth Corps, and Vegesack retained command of the Turners. The numbers in each of the regiments had so dwindled that the 21st New Jersey Regiment led by Gilliam Van Houten was added to our brigade to bring it up to strength. The 7th Maine Regiment was given leave, went home to recruit more volunteers, and returned in time to participate in battles around Fredericksburg.

From December, 1862 until May, 1863, the center of combat between the North and South in Virginia was around the towns of Fredericksburg and Chancellorsville. Many changes took place in the various commands of the Army of the Potomac. McClellan was dismissed. Subsequently, the army came under the leadership of General Ambrose Burnside, but, later, command was given to General Joseph Hooker.

It is impossible for me to give a detailed account of the participation of the 20th New York Regiment in the many battles which were fought during that period. I had been released from the hospital, but I was sent on leave; I stayed with Francesca and George Zell in Philadelphia. However, through correspondence with my comrades, I discovered that Sedgwick took command of the Sixth Corps by May, 1863. The Turners engaged the Rebels at Fredericksburg, Marye's Heights, Salem Church, and Chancellorsville. The outcome of all the campaigning during this time only appeared to favor the South heavily. In the battles, Lee and Jackson outmaneuvered the Federals, but the Confederates could never produce a "knockout punch." Likewise, no matter how hard they tried, the Union forces could not maintain an offensive. Neither side could dominate in this "bloody poker game!" The casualties were high and the South's greatest loss came with the death of General Thomas "Stonewall" Jackson following the battle of Chancellorsville.

The last engagement for the Turners was played out on a hill near Chancellorsville, during the first part of May, 1863. Then, General Thomas Neill was leading the Third Brigade of the Second Division in the Sixth Corps. The battle was disastrous for the brigade, especially for our 20th New York Regiment. The Third Brigade was stationed at the crest of a hill looking down into a ravine that had seen a day's battle. At 5 P.M., the rebel yell burst forth from the woods that bordered the bottom of the ravine. The Confederate infantry, 16,000 strong, began to charge toward the crest where only the Third Brigade stood in defense. Neill could have ordered it to fall down and fire from a prone position but, instead, he raised his sword and bellowed, "Forward, Third Brigade!" The men responded instantly and dashed down the hill toward the oncoming enemy. They charged into a "Valley of Death!" When it was over, 52 men had been killed, 394 were wounded, and 404 were missing.

In this battle, the Turners again broke ranks and went to the rear. In their retreat, they interfered with Captain James H. Rigby's Maryland Light Artillery unit. When the Rebels were 80 yards from his cannons Rigby shouted, "Limber to the rear!" However, his men could not carry out the command amid the confusion caused by the Turner's retreat. Suddenly, the horses used to drive one of Rigby's artillery pieces ran away. The cannon would have to be surrendered to the enemy if it could not be removed. Rigby brought forth his saber and with hard blows to the shoulders of the running Turners forced them to drag the field piece 200 yards to the rear. As this was being done the 3rd Vermont Regiment came up in support and drove the Rebels back.

I have often wondered why Vegesack could not rally and regroup the Turners at Chancellorsville, and I was disappointed that the regiment failed to keep the vow of fidelity which it made at Harrison's Landing in August, 1862. I can only surmise that the regiment's poor conduct was associated with a great fear of being destroyed only one month before its release from the service. If this was true, it is understandable. Recovering from my own wound at that time, I knew how to have sympathy for my comrades, and General Neill's order to charge, while being outnumbered by the Rebels, did seem to be ill conceived.

On May 30, 1863, the 20th and 33rd New York Regiments left the camp of the Sixth Corps and were transported to New York City. There, on June 3, 1863, our regiment was mustered out. Of the 1,200 healthy men who had left in 1861, only 694 "whole" persons returned. Nine officers and 122 enlisted men had died, 174 were missing, and 201 had received serious wounds. My Company B had been reduced to 38 privates. I believe you can understand the sadness which we had whenever we reminisced about the roll call which we gave at Staten Island on May 9, 1861.

I received an honorable medical discharge on April 30, 1863. I had received $11 per month from May, 1861 until August of that year. Then, it was increased to $13 per month. Upon privately saying farewell to one of my officers, I was given the bulk sum of $57.50 for a severance subsistence. With such a fanfare, my roll as der Turner Soldat was over!

"Morgenrot; Morgenrot leuchtest mir zum fruehen Tod!" Were the morning rays of our ideals worth the combat, wounds, and death? For many years I was troubled, but I think they were! For a quarter of a century, I enjoyed the economic and social benefits of a Union preserved. Realistically, being der Turner Soldat was a part of my life which I could not forget. My wound would not allow me to forget! On one hand, I was happy to have had these Civil War experiences; on the other hand, I would never desire to repeat them!

Newly appointed Brigadier General Max Weber bidding farewell to Lincoln, Stanton, Chase, and Wool as his troops leave Fortress Monroe for the attack on Norfolk, Virginia. The 20th New York Regiment was part of Weber's force. Drawing by Jack Clifton.

Top: At Yorktown, May, 1862. Clockwise from the left; Duc de Chartres, Prince de Joinville, and Comte de Paris. Bottom: Scene at Savage's Station on Richmond & York Railroad, June 28, 1862. Photograph by James Gibson.

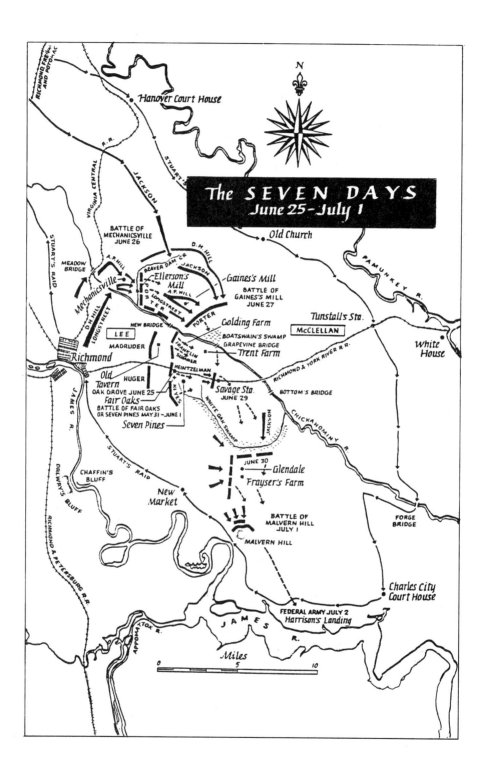

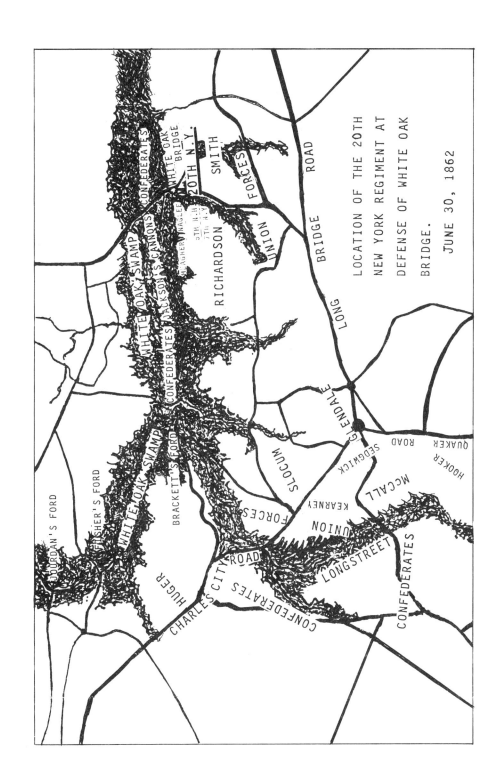

Scenes at Harrison's Landing, July and August, 1862. Top: The Berkley Mansion, McClellan's headquarters. Center: U.S. Mail Boat Wharf. Federal prisoners exchanged at Aiken's Landing disembarked here to rejoin their units. Bottom: Redouts near the Westover Church, constructed by the 20th New York Regiment.

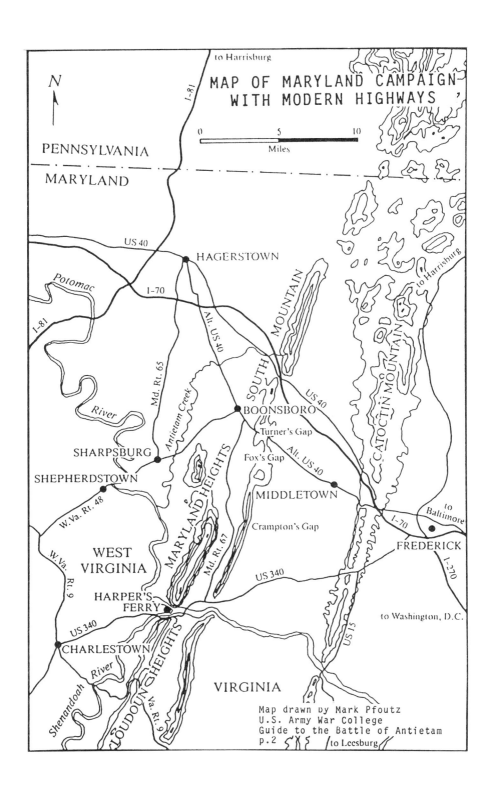

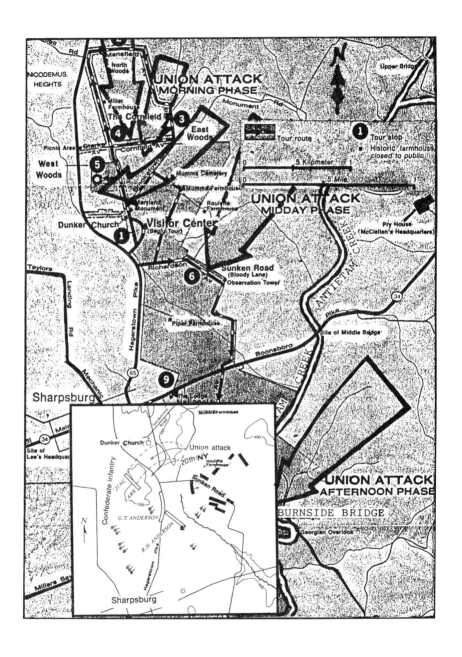

The National Park Service's tourist map of the Antietam battlefield. The insert at the bottom shows the position of the 20th New York Regiment when it first engaged the advancing Confederates (The 27th North Carolina Regiment and the 3rd Arkansas Regiment) on September 17, 1862. From whence, it drove the enemy back to Dunker church and held the high ground slightly to the north of the visitor center.

Edwin Forbes's battlefield sketch of the Charge on Dunker Church, September 17, 1862. Three regiments of the Third Brigade, Second Division, Sixth Corps led by William H. Irwin are illustrated (20th, 33rd, and 77th New York Regiments).

Scenes at Antietam. Top: View of the battlefield from the Pry House. The long column moving vertically across the field, between Mumma's burning farmhouse and the exploding caisson, is the Sixth Corps. The 20th New York Regiment leads the column. Bottom: Federal wounded at Mumma's farm. "The water in the spring was salty," said Futterer.

The Turner Rifles saw these scenes of death and destruction during its charge on Dunker Church. It was accompanied by the 33rd and 77th New York Regiments. The photographs were taken by Alexander Gardner on September 10, 1862, two days after the battle of Antietam.

Monuments at Antietam honoring the 20th New York Regiment. Left: Dedicated by the Turners in the National Cemetery, 1887. Right: Dedicated by the State of New York on the battlefield, 1912.

THE PRIVATE'S CHALLENGE

At the time of my discharge, I was given a two-thirds disability pension. I could not hear in my right ear, I could not sleep peacefully, and I was nauseated at times with pus forming in my mouth. I was dissatisfied with my pension, fought for a full disability, and received it. I was also disillusioned because I felt there was a lack of appreciation for my volunteered service. The true value of my effort was not to be judged by one battle but by my initial volunteering, my boarding of ships, my walking through swamps, my sweating, my feeling thirsty, my honoring every command, my suffering imprisonment, and my experiencing pain because of my wound. I had spent five months in the hospital, and my recovery was not complete. I did not perform my duty for an exorbitant pay; I was not a mercenary!

My regiment was mustered out. The war lingered on! We, who had served our term, seemed to be forgotten; our value was held suspect by the War Department! My disillusionment increased as I imagined that I was just one insignificant speck of color in the immense fresco of that war. I questioned, "If I am insignificant with regard to my own time, imagine how insignificant I will be as the months turn to years, years to decades, and decades to centuries!

Pliny the Younger, circa 100 A.D., remarked, "Since it is not granted us to live long, let us transmit to posterity some memorial that we have at least lived." I begot 11 children by my wife, Magdelena. Five lived to maturity: three boys and two girls. Through them, my verbal accounts of the war were transmitted to their children. Further, my letters written to my parents and sister also kept me "alive," since they were preserved intact into the 20th century. The Federal Government, through the War Department, preserved my military records. Now, after 125 years, anyone can discover the deeds of Erhard Futterer, der Turner Soldat. My Wanderbuch, which contains more details than a modern college transcript, was treasured by my youngest daughter. She saved it and passed it on to her daughter who, by interpreting its contents, determined my motivation for emigrating to America. Most of all, I was fortunate that someone had the interest and took the time to put the pieces together, forming a verbal fresco, which gives my regiment an exposure so long overdue, this exposure being made during the 125th anniversary of the Civil War.

In America, as the 20th century grows to a close, there are at least 50 descendants who are able to call me their great-great grandfather. Assuming that the survivors of my regiment were as prolific as I and as fortunate in having their children grow to maturity, there would be today at least 45,000 Americans who can claim as their great-great grandfather a member of The United Turner Rifles.

I challenge each of them to discover his or her great-great grandfather and help to embellish the story which I have begun. More reminiscences of the other members of Company B need to be recorded; an investigation into the lives of the men of the other nine companies is required. The military and political intrigue, seen with the eyes of those men, from the time of Antietam to the time of our muster-out, needs research; their homecomings, their feelings, and their civilian lives, before and after the war, should be investigated. How did their wounds affect their later lives? Were they satisfied with their pensions? What did they think of Francis Weiss? Where did he go after the war?

I also challenge the members of the American Turners in the East. Let the 20th New York Regiment's activities in the Civil War be, for the young members, Geistliches Turnen. As an outcome of their mental gymnastics, at least one member might "turn" my challenge into a Doctor of Philosophy thesis. Others, as amateur historians, can present their oratories at Civil War Round Tables in the United States and Canada or prepare publications for Civil War magazines and newspapers, which have proliferated in the country. The American Turners in the midwest can do the same. Recall, the 17th Missouri Regiment was the Turner Regiment of the West, and the 9th Ohio Regiment was completely composed of Turners from Cincinnati.

I consider my effort as just a beginning and I believe that my challenge will be accepted. Am I being too presumptuous? It has been said that Americans have little interest in history; they consider the past so irrelevant to their lives! However, I think the Civil War is and should be relevant to yours! Why you? You are the descendants of the immigrants who participated in it. More books have been written about it than any other period of American history and, proportionally, few of them are devoted to your ancestors!

Hang on to your roots! Accept my challenge! My comrades will be resurrected, my regimental history will be given scholarly attention, and all Turner regiments will become a greater part of American historical literature. Envision the avalanche of books and pamphlets, wonderful documents to be presented to America for the 150th anniversary of the Civil War in 2012 A.D.! What a beautiful fresco! What an honor to the American Turners everywhere!

"Gut Heil"

Erhard Futterer
Company B

THE AUTHORS' APOLOGIA

The dictionary defines apologia as a formal defense or justification. Although the story you have read, related by Futterer, may be considered a narration rather than a scholarly work, the facts related are based upon the translations of Futterer's letters and results obtained from a systematic search and interpretation of historical literature. As such, the authors do not feel that they need a formal justification of their work other than the bibliography at the end of the treatise. However, since there are facts about the United Turner Rifles, interesting and controversial, which could not be interwoven into the Futterer story, they thought that it was necessary to present a formal appendage to his account of the regiment's activities. Hence a chapter follows which is titled: "From Bits and Pieces." In this, Miller reveals his thoughts and emotions concerning the attention popular historians devote to the exploits of the 20th New York Regiment. He explains how and why he was motivated to prepare the narrative for consideration by the American Turners and others interested in the Civil War. This section has been placed in the treatise after the Futterer story. If presented before, he felt that the reader would become weary with the academics. In its present location, he feels that it embellishes the story.

FROM BITS AND PIECES

For many years after the Civil War, the surviving veterans of the 20th New York Volunteer Regiment, some of whom were members of the New York Turnverein, annually celebrated the anniversary of the battle of Antietam. They were joined in this celebration, rallying around their regimental flag, a tattered but sacred relic of the society, by the Turnschwestern. These were the survivors of the ladies auxiliary, who provided some clothing and equipment needs to outfit the regiment before they left New York in 1861. In 1920, the numbers in these two groups had so dwindled that they were forced to discontinue their activities.

The following year the Verein asked one of its distinguished members, Doctor Gustav Scholer, to take the flag, upon which was inscribed the phrase, Bahn Frei, to the New York State Military Museum in Albany, New York. Here it was to be preserved for posterity along with the regimental flags of other volunteer regiments from New York; Scholer died in 1928. He had served as First Speaker for the Verein from 1888 to 1902. Until his retirement, he was, as a physician, a coroner of New York City.

My "gut" feeling leads me to believe that the white flag, shown next to the Union flag in Edwin Forbes's drawing, depicting Irwin's charge on Dunker Church, is the Turner regimental flag. However, I have no proof. In the summer of 1986, I telephoned Camille O'Leary in Albany, New York. She is a curator of the New York Military Museum, in charge of cataloging the Civil War flag collection. She informed me that she was unable to locate the 20th New York Regiment's flag and was surprised that it had not been returned to the State immediately after the war. In August, 1987, at a dinner meeting with Hans Sammer, who was acting chairman of the Jahn Fund and is a prominent member of the New York Turnverein, I was informed that volumes of documentation concerning the activities of the 20th New York Regiment were destroyed in the Turnverein's move from Yorkville to its present location in the Bronx near Throgs Neck. The inability to locate memorabilia, like the flag and documents, made investigative work leading to the reconstruction of the regimental history frustrating.

The New York Turnverein was founded in 1850, eleven years prior to the American Civil War. The *Historical Journal; Centennial Celebration*, a souvenir of the 100th anniversary of the Turnverein's founding, was written in 1950. One section was devoted to honoring the participation of the Verein members who fought in that war which was called, by the Germans, the Buergerkrieg. Recollections of some of the survivors, orally related before their death, were included in the *Journal.* Knowledge of these illustrates how small tidbits of private information, when cross referenced with facts from historical documents, help to embellish the events in which the veterans participated.

Such is particularly true concerning the regiment's charge on Dunker Church at Antietam. One veteran recalls how General William F. Smith, observing the fierce fighting of the Confederates with the retreating

Federals at the Mumma farm, bellowed, "Put that German regiment to the front!" Another recalls that Smith said, "Fix your bayonets, boys!" From these remarks, we can see that there was hand-to-hand fighting before the charge began. Several other veterans dramatized the subsequent action. They said, "Exposed to heavy fire, our regimental banner, Bahn Frei, was held high as shot and shell slashed the corn field and lacerated our bodies." They also recalled that, on this occasion, Irwin was at the head of the charge instructing his troops, "Fire Low Today, 20th; Fire Low!" It is statements like these that agree with the description of the 20th New York Regiment's participation as given in *Following the Greek Cross* and selections taken from Vol II of *Battles and Leaders of the Civil War*. If only more of these personal accounts had been preserved, our task of reconstructing the regimental history would have been facilitated.

Although I was motivated to reconstruct the regimental history because my wife's grandfather, Erhard Futterer, was known to be a member of Company B, I found little information to begin my task other than what was in his war record. The only account which I could consider close to a regimental history was a 12 page article, published in 1906, in the *Lehigh Railroad Magazine,* entitled, "The 20th Regiment, New York Volunteers, Take Veterans Tour of Battlefields." I was able to find this article on microfilm under the code *ZH-IAG*, only in the New York City Public Library. It was written on the occasion of the Railroad's endorsed, personally conducted, tour for the veterans to Gettysburg, Antietam, Harper's Ferry, and Washington D.C., from the 9th to the 15th of September in 1906. This was the last formal tour that the survivors made, to see once again the places where their comrades fought, were wounded, and died, from 1861 to 1863. It was the occasion of the 45th anniversary of their induction into service.

At Antietam they had an opportunity to see the monument which they, through their personal finance, had erected in the National Cemetery. As they gazed upon the structure they saw a block of granite nine feet high topped with a sculptured collage of a wreath and the paraphernalia of their comrades: drum and drumsticks, forage cap, canteen, knapsack, and cartridge box, all mounted on a formidable base. On one side of the base inscribed in German is, "ZUM ANDENKEN AN UNSERE GEFALLENEN KAMARADEN ERRICHTET VON UEBERLEBENDEN DES REGTS." On the opposite side is the English translation: "IN REMEMBRANCE TO OUR FALLEN COMRADES ERECTED BY THE SURVIVORS OF THE REGIMENT." The third side has a cross indented into the granite; below it is written: 20th REGIMENT, N.Y. VOLS., TURNER RIFLES, 3rd BRIGADE, 2nd DIV., 6th CORPS, 1861-1863. Directly under this inscription, protruding from the surface, is the Ogling Owl, expressing "Gut Heil." The final side carries the phrase, DEDICATED, SEPTEMBER 17, 1887. This was the 25th anniversary of the "Bloodiest

Day." When I first saw this date, on my visit to the battlefield in 1980, I was confused. The *Historical Journal; Centennial Celebration* claims that the monument was erected in 1912, on the occasion of the 50th anniversary of the Antietam Battle. I have concluded that the *Journal* is in error.

Further research uncovered other errors. The *Journal*, contends that the 20th New York Regiment skirmished at Black River, Virginia. In actuality, the regiment skirmished at Back River Creek. It erroneously reports Colonel Weber's promotion to the rank of brigadier general in June, 1862 instead of April, 1862. In April, Baron von Vegesack did not assume command of the regiment, as the *Journal* claims. Francis Weiss was chosen by the Turners as its leader. Also, the *Journal* leads one to believe that the Turners supplied the regiment's entire needs; the New York State *Annual Report of the Commissary General of Ordnance for the Year 1861* reveals that the State provided it with rifles, bayonets, cartridge boxes, waist belts and plates, cap pouches and picks, bayonet scabbard and frogs, gun slings, knapsacks, haversacks, and canteens. The Turnschwestern supplied underclothing and accouterments not provided by the State. Finally, the *Journal* presents a picture of a partially completed monument erected, by the State of New York, at the precise spot on which the regiment stood in combat at Antietam. Today, a top portion ending in a pointed apex completes the structure.

Discrepancies such as these may have hindered the task of reconstruction, but having to search through so many sources, where only bits and pieces pertain to the 20th New York Regiment, made the job Herculean. The labyrinth of such sources includes *The War of the Rebellion: A Compilation of Official Records of the Union and Confederate Armies*, books and articles about regiments that fought beside the 20th New York Regiment, literary works specializing in the participation of foreign troops in the Civil War, and pamphlets, magazines, and newspapers containing information seemingly unrelated to the 20th New York Regiment. In making the journey through this labyrinth, I felt, many times, like the Curies, extracting so small a residue of radium from a large bulk of pitchblend.

In a pamphlet, entitled *The Battlefield of Antietam*, I found a compilation of stories told to Oliver T. Reilly. He was for five decades, extending into the 20th century, the official guide to the battlefield. He recorded his conversations with veterans and other eyewitnesses who visited the site. At first, these stories appeared to contribute little to my assigned task, but after my cross referencing them with other documented and personal recollections, they became a source of enlightenment.

In one story, Reilly told of Jacob Lair, a member of the 20th New York Regiment, visiting the battlefield in 1906; he found some grape shot on the spot where he had his arm blown away in the charge on Dunker Church. The discovery emotionally moved him! When this revelation was cross referenced with events in Erhard Futterer's life, it was discovered that Lair was, in fact, Jacob Leier of Company B and a comrade of Futterer.

For two weeks after the battle, they both had their wounds attended to in a field hospital set up at the Hoffman farm, northeast of the East Woods near Smoketown. From there, they were moved to Hagerstown and shipped to a hospital in Baltimore.

Reilly relates another story which, at first, appears to have no relation to the 20th New York Regiment. On the day of the Antietam battle, the spring at Mumma's farm was polluted. Some accused the Confederates of deliberately placing salt in the water as a pernicious act. However, Samuel Mumma Jr. told Reilly that his father had gone into Hagerstown the day before the battle and purchased several bags of salt. Upon returning, he placed these on the wooden floor in the barn above the spring. When the barn burned, during the morning hours of the battle, the bags fell into the spring, polluting it. The story gives verification to one of the statements made by Futterer who said, "After I had been wounded in the charge on Dunker Church, some of my comrades helped me back to Mumma's farm. There I bathed my wound in water which was very salty."

On reviewing some literature concerning the dramatic club of the New York Turnverein I discovered Othelia Gehrt. She was a remarkable actress who died at an advanced age in 1912. She accompanied the 20th New York Regiment, during a considerable part of its field actions, as a nurse and camp attendant. Leier and Futterer recalled how she accompanied them and other wounded when they were sent to Baltimore.

Since some authors, who present brief sketches of the United Turner Rifles in their writings, appear to know little about the Turner Movement, it is understandable that some of their interpretations are erroneous. Ella Lonn, professor of history at Goucher College, in her book, *Foreigners in the Union Army and Navy*, claims that the Turner regiments served in the military out of a spirit of adventure. This is an erroneous interpretation in light of the political philosophy and general principles held by the Turners prior to the war. Walter C. Eberhardt, director of physical education at St. Louis University, in his pamphlet, *The American Turners; Their Philosophy and Contributions to American Democracy*, written in 1955 says, "No matter where we look the Turners never feared to let people know their stand on the side of freedom: freedom of expression, freedom of speech, freedom of press, freedom of assembly, freedom of religious worship, freedom from exploitation, and freedom from oppression." This intense desire for freedom and a strong willingness to defend it is expressed by a German officer, who was a Turner and member of a Missouri regiment, in *The Crisis*, a Civil War novel written by Winston Churchill in 1901. In 1855, at the Turner convention in Buffalo, New York, the Turners took upon themselves to publicly denounce slavery. In 1860, they played an active role in campaigning for the election of Abraham Lincoln and, through the German press, expressed their favor for the Republican Party and the progressive ideals that it favored. Imbued with such sentiments, it is understandable that, when Lincoln called for 75,000 militia on

April 15, 1861, the Turners responded quickly but not out of a spirit of adventure. Theirs was a spirit to preserve the Union and the Constitution as they knew it.

Late in April, 1861, the First Speaker of the New York Turnverein, Rudolph Kluckhuhn, prepared a proclamation. He announced that the Vereine of New York and Williamsburg felt it their duty to answer the call to arms. Further, he expressed the conviction that, with their cry, Bahn Frei, they could strike a blow to aid the victory of justice, freedom, and the Constitution. The proclamation was given in a special meeting at the Turnhalle. The meeting room was jammed to capacity. Before the evening ended, the Vereine had formed a war committee which consisted of Kluckhuhn, Bernet, Lorch, Bennecke, and Hoyn. The following week the regiment was created and Max Weber, an immigrant Acht-und-vierziger and former soldier in the Baden revolutionary army of 1848, was elected as its commander. He received the rank of colonel. Subsequent activities of the regiment that were of public interest were reported in several newspapers, particularly in the *New York Herald* and the *Chicago Staats-Zeitung*.

In my investigation, I found authors who were biased or prejudiced. In *Battles and Leaders* Rush C. Hawkins, who before the war ended was raised to the rank of brigadier general, describes the amphibious attack of the army and navy at Hatteras Inlet. He does not acknowledge that detached units of the 20th New York Regiment, of which Company B was one, played a major role in this invasion. Hawkins, who was a colonel at the time of the Hatteras incident, led the 9th New York Zouaves. At the conclusion of reading his article you would think that his troops played the major role, and the 20th New York Regiment, by chance, was also there. His account first appeared in 1887. In 1963, John G. Barrett, in his book, *The Civil War in North Carolina*, tells a much different story. The ship that carried the Zouaves was grounded and the majority of their numbers like those of the Turners did not land during the battle. The *Official Records* states that 102 Turners were able to overcome the hazards of the rough waves and rally on shore, accompanied by units of the Union Coast Guard, the 2nd U.S. Artillery, and 68 of Hawkin's Zouaves. However, the Zouaves were led by Captain Jardine, not Hawkins.

All through Civil War literature, written by nativistic eyewitnesses, I found prejudice toward the Germans and much of it has been perpetuated by modern authors' quoting and requoting these eyewitnesses. The German officers were criticized. Why? They were not graduates of West Point, they could not trace their lineage back to the Revolutionary War, and they spoke in broken English. When excited on the battlefield, they sometimes forgot their English and gave all their commands in German. However, a language problem does not imply a lack of military ability, and not all West Pointers were great officers.

The enlisted men were considered, by nativistic officers, as mere attachments to "our" army; it was as if they were on loan from a European nation. They were accused of drinking, stealing, and cheating, actions which they performed no more than, but as much as, their nativistic American and English-speaking immigrant counterparts. Many times, guilty nativistic Union soldiers, after being suspected of despoiling and ravaging, would respond accusingly, "The Germans did it. They always do it. You can't trust them."

At first, it may not be understandable why this prejudice should have existed, but the Germans, being a very sizable minority, may have been thought of by others as a threat. The Germans were the largest immigrant contingent in the Union army, followed by the Irish. A.B. Faust in his book, *The German Element in the United States,* shows that it was conceivable that one out of every three men in the army was of German ancestry. It was remarked that General Lee once said, "Take the Dutch out of the Union army and we could whip those Yankees easily!"

However, prejudice persisted long after the war, a prejudice kept alive by "American" officers who were the authors of the bulk of literature which rendered eyewitness accounts of the war years. Many of these accounts were a defense of their author's decisions and actions during the war.

On June 15, 1901, General Max Weber died at his home at 458 Willoughby Avenue, Brooklyn, New York. The next day General Rush Hawkins cut his obituary from the newspaper and placed it in a scrapbook, which has been preserved in Ann Mary Brown Memorial Library at Brown University. Next to the inserted obituary Hawkins wrote, "Weber, although not a great soldier as at first his friends claimed he would turn out to be, was an earnest and intelligent commanding officer. He was moderate and made one of the better records among the Germans who entered our service. His fair reputation was honestly earned." This is indeed faint praise for the man who fought so fiercely, in General William French's division, at Antietam where, as a noble officer, he received a shattered arm in leading his brigade in a charge on the Sunken Road.

Another example of discrimination against a foreigner involves Ernst Mattais Peter von Vegesack, a Swedish citizen. He led the 20th New York Regiment from July, 1862 to June, 1863. Vegesack fought heroically at Gaines's Mill, Antietam, Fredericksburg, Chancellorsville, and Gettysburg. He was refused promotion to the rank of brigadier general even though Count Piper, of the Swedish Legation in Washington, had interceded for him. Disappointed, he resigned his commission and returned to Sweden before the war ended. Not until 1893 was he awarded the Congressional Medal of Honor for his services in the Civil War.

His being rejected for promotion may be connected to the alleged accusations of misconduct that have engulfed the 20th New York Regiment even to the present time. If the administration had rewarded the man, it would have had to reward the troops he led. In an 1865 document which I found at Fortress Monroe, on my visit there in 1985, serious accusations of misconduct of the enlisted men of the 20th New York Regiment are recorded; they were accused of running and skulking during the battle at White Oak Swamp and breaking ranks during General Thomas Neill's attempted repulse of General Longstreet's Confederates at Chancellorsville. These accusations, being unresolved, were delaying completion of the regiment's records. The *Official Records* tells us of the dismissals of officers and change of commands that took place in Smith's division after it had retreated to Harrison's Landing. Both Hyde *(Following the Greek Cross)* and Thomas Livermore *(The Blue and the Gray)* report the Germans' breaking ranks and running during the defense of White Oak Swamp. Further, prisoner records show that a large number of men from the 20th New York Regiment were incarcerated on Belle Isle after the Seven Days Battle of 1862.

In 1985, my wife and I made an exhaustive study of the area around the White Oak Swamp Bridge where the allegedly discrediting event took place, at "high noon" on June 30, 1862. Our findings, coupled with a plausible organization of the facts in the literature, indicate that confusion, military dress, terrain, and dereliction of duty on the part of one officer caused humiliation for the entire regiment. Further, in Wilhelm Kaufmann's book, *Die Deutschen im amerikanischen Buergerkriege*, I discovered that the delinquent officer was Colonel Francis Weiss. Kaufmann says sarcastically, "He was a shirker of duty and 'distinguished' himself in the bloody battle of White Oak Swamp by his absence!" I believe that, in Erhard Futterer's narration, an excellent case has been made to show that circumstance played a large role in that unfortunate situation, and the enlisted men had little to be ashamed of. In regimental histories which I have read, written by eyewitnesses, heroics have been emphasized. Human frailty, confusion resulting from shabby command, and lack of experience had to be hidden. Today we are detached, investigatively not emotionally involved. In Futterer's narration, I have attempted to show that intelligent action in face of an impossible situation does not have to be equated to running or skulking. However, in the future, it is expected that the American Turners, accepting the *Private's Challenge,* will be leaders in presenting a scholarly determination of the reasons for and the interpretation of the regiment's alleged poor conduct. Partictularly, a true scholarly work on their part would include a detailed investigation of Francis Weiss and the leadership role of Ernst von Vegesack at Chancellorsville.

It is tragic that no one, during the past 125 years, has revealed in a scholarly treatise the true exploits of the 20th New York Regiment, the United Turner Rifles. Time-Life Books recently published 27 popular volumes, *A Complete Library of the Civil War.* In all those volumes only a single phrase is devoted to the Turner Rifles. In *Rebels Resurgent,* one volume of this library describing the battle at Fredericksburg and Salem Church in 1863, the author, Goolrick, states, "Two brigades of Early's division pushed westward as planned, throwing the 20th New York and an artillery unit back in confusion." Readers interested in the United Turner Rifles would have spent approximately $460 to be so niggardly enlightened.

An advantage which I had in producing this narration was access to translations of Futterer's letters. In 1974 and 1979, my wife and I traveled to Forchheim, West Germany, the birthplace of Erhard Futterer. We found that my wife had a cousin living in the village. This cousin's grandmother and Erhard Futterer were siblings. The former stayed in Germany when Erhard and his other sister, Francesca, emigrated to America in 1855. The letters which Futterer wrote to his parents and sister were saved and passed down to the cousin, Ernst Fehr. On our visits, these letters, written in German script, were translated for us by the villagers. The contents were a decided help in my detective work, my piecing together of the facts found in the American literature.

Combining all the bits and pieces, I feel that Steinlage and I have put together an accurate but, admittedly, incomplete military history of the United Turner Rifles. We allowed Futterer to tell the story. We know he could not have been knowledgeable of all the events and situations we allowed him to narrate, but we envisioned him to be der Turner Soldat as Bell Irvin Wiley did with Billy Yank.

You have read the story and we believe you have found the motives of the Turners to be pure and idealistic. They were men who loved their adopted country and their newly found freedom; they despised dictatorship. They were ordinary men subject to human frailty, but, like ordinary men doing ordinary things in an extraordinary manner, they achieved greatness. One might consider their charge on Dunker Church, during the battle of Antietam, to be the high point of their military history. It happened on September 17, 1862, exactly 75 years to the day of the signing of the American Constitution, the document which, in April, 1861, First Speaker Kluckhuhn asked the Turners to defend by force of arms.

Hence, in spite of a lost flag and documents, disparaging insinuations by eyewitnesses, failure of popular historians to promote proper credits, and the Federal Government's procrastination in making a deserved award, we believe that you have read a story which has honored the men of the 20th New York Regiment without hiding their human frailty. It is a story which proudly and honestly gives them their rightful place in American history.

BIBLIOGRAPHY

Baden Department of the Interior, *Grossherzoglich badisches Wanderbuch #2931* Karlsruhe, West Germany, 1852. Copy in the Futterer collection of C. Eugene Miller and Marie M. Miller, 202 Wildwood Lane, Louisville, Kentucky.
Bailey, Ronald H., *The Bloodiest Day; The Battle of Antietam*, Time-Life Books, Alexandria, Virginia, 1984.
Barrett, John G., *The Civil War in North Carolina*, University of North Carolina Press, Chapel Hill, 1963.
Barrett, John G., *North Carolina as a Civil War Battleground*, North Carolina Department of Cultural Resources, Raleigh, 1984.
Binder, Hedwig, *Die ab-und Auswanderung von Forchheim am Kaiserstuhl waehrend des 19. Jahrunderts*, Forchheim, West Germany, 1970.
Brommwell, William J., *History of Immigration to the United States*, A. M. Kelly Publications, New York, 1969.
Burn, James D., *Three Years Among the Working Classes in the United States During the War*, Smith and Elden, London, 1865.
Castle, (editors), *Battles and Leaders of the Civil War*, (four vols.), Castle Book Sales Inc., Secaucus, N.J., 1983.
Catton, Bruce, *Mr. Lincoln's Army*, Doubleday and Company Inc., New York, 1962.
Churchill, Winston, *The Crisis*, The Copp, Clark Company Ltd., Toronto, Canada, 1901.
Commager, Henry S., *The Blue and the Gray*, Fairfax Press, New York, 1982.
Cooke, Adrian, *The Armies of the Streets; New York Draft Riots in 1863*, University of Kentucky Press, Lexington, Kentucky, 1974.
Davis, William C., *Civil War Parks; The Story Behind the Scenery*, KC Publications Inc., (in cooperation with the Eastern National Park & Monument Assoc.), Las Vegas, Nevada, 1984.
Dowdey, Clifford, *The Great Plantation*, Berkley Plantation, Charles City, Virginia, 1980.
Eberhardt, Walter C., *The American Turners; Their History, Philosophy and Contributions to American Democracy*, Indiana University, Bloomington, Indiana, 1955.
Faust A.B., *The German Element in the United States*, (see Kaufmann W., *Die Deutsch. im amerikan. Buergerkrieg.)* Boston and New York, 1909.
Franz, Eugen, *Muenchen als deutsche Kulturstadt im 19. Jahrunderts*, W. de Gruyter Co., Berlin, 1936.
Frassanito, William A., *Antietam*, Charles Scribner's Sons, New York, 1978.
French, H.F., *The Country Gentleman*, vol. 24, July 21, 1864.
Futterer, Erhard, *Letters to Forchheim*, the Futterer collection of Ernst Fehr, Kronnenstrasse, 7831 Forchheim, West Germany.
Gemeinde Forchheim, *Forchheim am Kaiserstuhl; Zum 1225-jaehrigen Jubilaeum seiner urkundlichen Ersterwaehnung*, Druckerei Emil Wild KG, Endingen, 1987.

Goolrick, William K., *Rebels Resurgent; Fredericksburg to Chancellorsville,* Time-Life Books, Alexandria, Virginia, 1985.
Guernsey, Alfred H., and Alden, Henry M., *Harper's History of the Great Rebellion,* Harper and Brothers, New York, 1866.
Halsey, Ashley Jr., *Who Fired the First Shot? and Other Stories of the Civil War,* Hawthorn Books Inc., New York, 1963.
Hansen, Marcus L., *The Immigrant in American History,* Harper and Row Co., New York, 1940.
Hansen, Marcus L., *The Atlantic Migration,* Harvard University Press, Cambridge, Mass., 1940.
Hawkins, R.C., *Private Papers and Scrapbook,* Ann Mary Brown Memorial Library Collection, Brown University, Providence, R.I.
Headley, Joel Tyler, *The Great Riots of New York; 1712-1873,* New York Clover Publication, New York, 1971.
Herberts, Kurt, *Artists Techniques,* (translated from the German, *Die Maltechniken,* Econ-Verlag im Duesseldorf), Frederick A. Prager Co., New York, 1958.
Hyde, Thomas W., *Following the Greek Cross,* The Riverside Press, (electrotyped and printed by H.O. Houghten & Co.), Cambridge, Mass., 1894.
Kaufmann, Wilhelm, *Die Deutschen im amerikanischen Buergerkriege* (sezessionskrieg 1861-1865), Druck und Verlag von R. Oldenburg, Muenchen und Berlin, 1911.
Lachouque, Henry and Brown, Anne S.K., *The Anatomy of Glory,* Arms and Armour Press, London/Melbourne, 1978.
Leech, Margaret, *Reveille in Washington; 1860-1865,* Time Reading; Special Edition, Time Inc., New York, 1941.
Lehigh Railroad, "20th Regiment New York Volunteers Take Veterans Tour of Battlefields," *Lehigh Railroad Magazine,* Microfilm; New York Public Library ZH-IAG, New York, 1906.
Leland, Charles G., *The Knickerbocker,* vol. 58, New York, August 1861. pp. 154-157.
Lonn, Ella, *Foreigners in the Confederacy,* University of North Carolina Press, Chapel Hill, 1963.
Lonn, Ella, *Foreigners in the Union Army and Navy,* Greenwood Press, New York, 1951.
Luvass, Jay and Nelson, Harold W., *The U.S. Army War College; Guide to the Battle of Antietam,* South Mountain Press Inc., Carlisle, Pa., 1987.
McNeill, B.D., *The Hatterasmen,* J.F. Blair Co., Winston-Salem, N.C., 1958.
Metzner, Henry, *History of the American Turners,* National Council of the American Turners, 3rd Revised Edition, Rochester, New York, 1974.
Military Records Service, NNCC, *Erhard Futterer's Civil War and Post Civil War Records,* National Archives, GSA, Washington D.C., 20408.

Murfin, James V., *The Gleam of Bayonets*, Thomas Yoseloff, New York, 1965.

New York State, *Annual Report of Commissary General of Ordnance for the Year 1861*, , Albany, New York, 1862. p-124.

New York State, *Annual Report of Commissary General of Ordnance for the Year 1862* Albany, New York, 1862. p-41.

New York State Bureau of Military Records, *Third Annual Report of the Chief of the Bureau of Military Records of New York State; February 2, 1866*, Albany, New York, 1866.

New York Turnverein, *Historical Journal; Centennial Celebration*, New York Turnverein Office, New York, 1950.

Palfrey, Francis W., *The Army in the Civil War*, vol. V., The Antietam and Fredericksburg, Charles Scribner's Sons, New York, 1881.

Phisterer, Frederick, *Statistical Record of the Armies of the United States*, Scribner's Sons, New York, 1883.

Phisterer, Frederick, *New York in the War of Rebellion*, Scribner's Sons, New York, 1885.

Pressly, Thomas J., *Americans Interpret Their Civil War*, The Free Press (Macmillan Pub. Co.), New York, 1965.

Price, William H., *Civil War Handbook*, Prince Lithograph Co., Fairfax, Virginia, 1961.

Reilly, Oliver T., *The Battlefield of Antietam*, Hagerstown Book Binding and Printing Co., Hagerstown, Md., 1906.

Rosengarten, Joseph, *The German Soldier in the Wars of the United States*, (see Kaufmann W., *Die Deutsch. im amerikan. Buergerkrieg)*, Philadelphia, Pa., 1886.

Sears, Stephen W., *Landscape Turned Red*, Ticknor and Fields, New Haven and New York, 1983.

Shannon Fred A., *The Organization and Administration of the Union Army 1861-1865*, vol. 2., Cleveland, Ohio, 1928. (A collection retained at the Troy, New York, Public Library)

Starke, Roger and Mohr, William D., *20th New York Volunteer Infantry Regiment (United Turner Rifles); 1861-1863; Plate No. 530.*, (source is Starke's reference to Dr. James Milgram Collection), Buffalo Historical Society, Buffalo, New York, 1974.

Stevens, George T., *The 6th Corps of the U.S. Army*, 2nd. ed., D. Van Nostrand, New York, 1870.

Symons, Jelinger C., *Arts and Artisans at Home and Abroad*, , Neill and Company, Old Fishmarket, Edinburgh, Scotland, 1839.

Tilberg, Frederick, *Antietam, National Park Service Series #31*, Washington D.C., 1960., revised 1961, reprint 1980.

United States Government, *The War of the Rebellion; A Compilation of the Official Records of the Union and Confederate Armies*, (129 vols., brief description: *Official Records*), Government Printing Office, Washington, D.C., 1887.

Watts, Anna Mary (Howitt), *An Art Student in Munich*, Ticknor, Reed and Fields, Boston, 1854.
Weber, Max, *The National Cyclopaedia of American Biography,* , vol. 12., p.264.
Weinert, Richard P., and Arthur, Robert, *Defenders of the Chesapeake; the Story of Fort Monroe,* Leeward Publications Inc., Annapolis, Md., 1978.
West, George B., *When the Yankees Came,* Parke Rouse Jr. ed., The Dietz Press, Richmond, Virginia, 1977.
Williams, Harry T., *Lincoln and His Generals,* Alfred A. Knopf Inc., New York, 1952.
Wiley, Bell Irwin, *The Life of Billy Yank,* Louisiana State University Press, Baton Rouge, 1983.
Wiley, Bell Irwin, *The Life of Johnny Reb,* Louisiana State University Press, Baton Rouge, 1893.
Zucker, A.E., *The Forty-Eighters,* Columbia University Press, New York, 1950.